Roses, Origami & Math

Roses, Origami & Math

Toshikazu Kawasaki

Translated by Kazuhiko Nagai

© 2005 English tex., Japan Publications Trading Co., Ltd.,
English edition by Japan Publications Trading Co., Ltd.,
1-2-1, Sarugaku-cho, Chiyoda-ku, Tokyo 101-0064, Japan.

Original Japanese edition published by Morikita Shuppan Co., Ltd.,
Tokyo, Japan in 1998 entitled "BARA TO ORIGAMI TO SUUGAKU TO"
© Toshikazu Kawasaki

First edition, First printing : March 2005

Distributors:
United States: Kodansha America, Inc. through Oxford University Press,
    198 Madison Avenue, New York, NY 10016, U.S.A.
Canada: Fitzhenry and Whiteside Ltd.,
    195 Allstates Parkway, Markham Ontario, L3R 4T8.
Australia and New Zealand: Bookwise International Pty Ltd.,
    174 Cormack Road, Wingfield, South Australia, Australia.
Asia and Japan: Japan Publications Trading Co., Ltd.,
    1-2-1, Sarugaku-cho, Chiyoda-ku, Tokyo 101-0064, Japan.

ISBN-13: 978-4-88996-184-3
ISBN-10: 4-88996-184-4

Printed in Japan

Orizuru (P.136)

Rose (P.129)

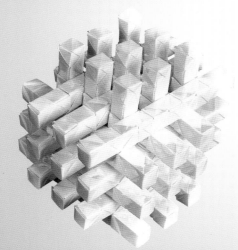

Hexagonal Construction (P.113)

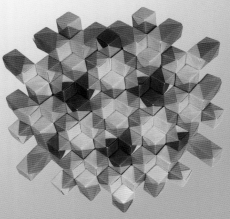

Hexagonal Construction (P.113)

Twist Construction (P.100)

Rose (P.129)

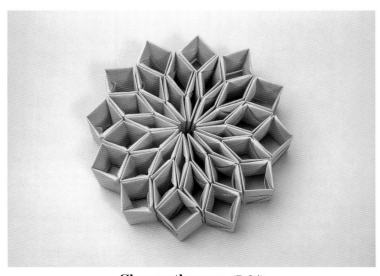

Chrysanthemum (P.34)

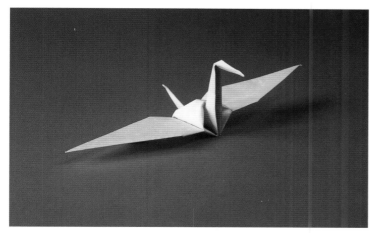

Generalized Bird (kite shape) (P.152)

Generalized Bird (turtle-crane) (P.172)

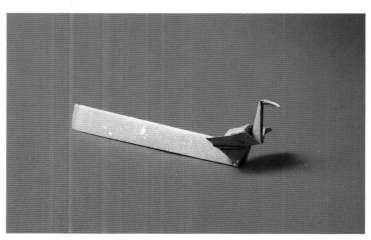

Generalized Bird (turtle-crane) (P.172)

Generalized Bird (open kite shape) (P.168)

Origami modules   Winter Scenery — A medieval townscape, the house of a feudal lord and the church being surrounded by houses —

FOREWORD

First of all, allow me to introduce myself. I came across origami in my high school days (15 – 18 years old). Since then the person who has been devoted to origami for 40 years is me. I met, loved and married my wife. The married life has continued almost 30 years. The first 10 years were full of pleasant memories, but in the course of 15, 20, and 25 years, there were not a few times when we had quarrels and shut our mouths and stayed silent. As far as origami is concerned, however, I have never lost the enthusiasm for the past 40 years. Should origami be the arts that only seek lyrical formation, it may have weakened my enthusiasm.

Luckily, I have been blessed with a lot of people with the same interests, who taught me the wide range of interesting points of origami. For the past 40 years, they have continued to arouse my enthusiasm further. Among them, the person who has demonstrated fantastic works, which stirred up my enthusiasm, one after another is the author of this book, Toshikazu Kawasaki.

So far I have published a lot of origami books. Among them, those that seem well written are the books motivated by Kawasak's masterpieces. The first on the list of his masterpieces is the well-known "Kawasaki's Roses." This book includes some works, which I introduced from the book to the public, in more refined forms. These works are by no means easy to fold. But this book begins with very simple examples, so try to master the basics of origami first of all, and then challenge them. If you succeed in making the exquisite roses bloom by your hand, you will certainly be acknowledged as advanced student.

Incidentally, Kawasaki is a mathematician by profession. Accordingly, the 'mathematical truth hidden in the depth of origami' is explained in the latter half of this book. You must be amazed to read the articles. Here is the most of the interesting points I mentioned above. Anyway, this is Kawasaki's first book long awaited by many origami lovers. You may feel like exclaiming "this is what I have been looking for!" I am certain that a large number of origami enthusiasts like me will come out inspired by this book.

Origami artist
Kunihiko Kasahara

PREFACE

A quarter of a century has passed since I was deeply involved in origami. For the past several years, I have been keenly aware of a thing. It is a great possibility that origami has. Every time I see people who are absorbed in folding origami, I feel that we will be able to make the best use of origami for education, and I do hope more people will enjoy the pleasure of origami.

This book consists of independent three parts. You may start reading from any parts which evoke your interest. There are also some practices are included. Beginners and origami lovers may try them by themselves to test their understanding, and teachers may make use of them in their classes. The problems of modules in part 1 are, particularly, intended to help understand the 'symmetry.' If you master them, they will ensure you to solve problems of mathematics skillfully.

Introduced in part 2 are methods of folding 3D roses from a sheet of paper without using scissors. The special techniques such as 'twist fold' and '3D twist fold' are important bases for Hiraoir and crystallographic origami, and you have to master them by all means.

Part 3 is the geometry of origami. The geometry explained is of junior high school level (the Pythagorean theorem, the inner center of a triangle, etc.). Even if you are not good at mathematics, try to fold the development charts of generalized birds in chapter 4. You will understand Orizuru's profundity and interesting points.

Toshikazu Kawasaki

CONTENTS

Chapter 2 Geometrical Form

Chapter 2 Flat Folding Condition

Chapter 3 Mountain-fold Crease and Valley-fold Crease

Chapter 4 The Geometry of Orizuru

Part I Modules

Chapter 1 Modules and Houses

1.1 Modules
Basic Module A
Cyrinder Module C
Simple Module B
Kite Module K

BASIC MODULE A (P2×4)

First of all, let's fold basic modules. There are two kinds of modules with four components (**bill** and **semi-bill**). Ordinary origami paper (**P1**=6"/15 cm square) makes a large module (square box), 5 1/8"/13.6 cm high, 2 3/4"/6.8 cm deep and wide. If you use paper for a small crane (**P2**=8"/7.5 cm square), you can make a suitable module.

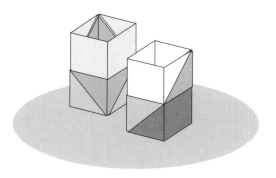

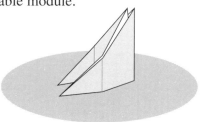

BILL (P2)

A component of **Basic Module A.**

Use yellow paper.

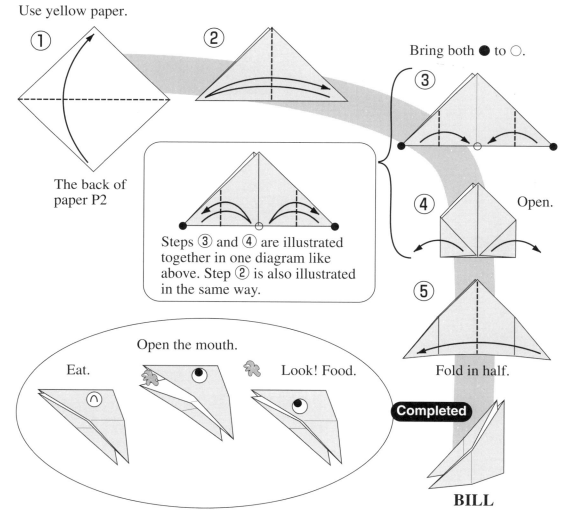

① The back of paper P2

②

Bring both ● to ○.

③

Steps ③ and ④ are illustrated together in one diagram like above. Step ② is also illustrated in the same way.

④ Open.

⑤ Fold in half.

Completed

Open the mouth.

Eat.   Look! Food.

BILL

SEMI-BILL (P2)

This component resembles the bill. Steps ❶-❻ show how to fold, but ❶ ②-④ will be easy to understand the whole.

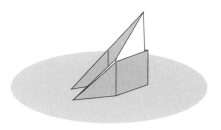

Use red paper.

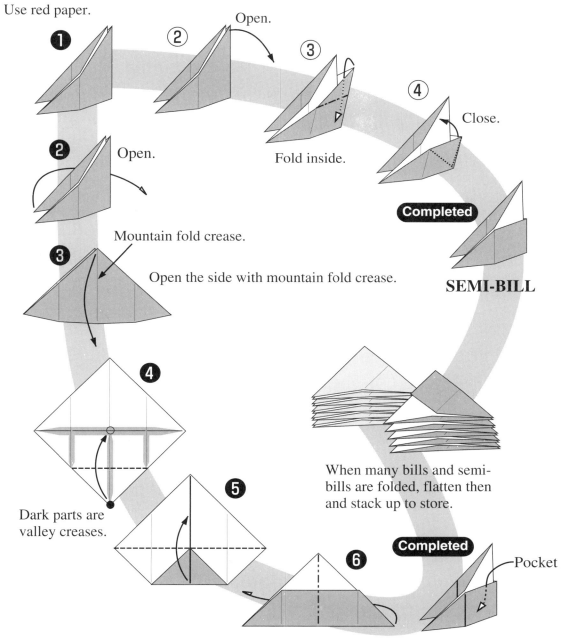

❶

② Open.

③ Fold inside.

④ Close.

Completed

SEMI-BILL

❷ Open.

❸ Mountain fold crease.

Open the side with mountain fold crease.

❹ Dark parts are valley creases.

❺

❻

When many bills and semi-bills are folded, flatten then and stack up to store.

Completed

Pocket

SEMI-BILL

Problem 1-1: Select correct **Bills** and **Semi-bills**. Point out the wrong parts of incorrect modeles.

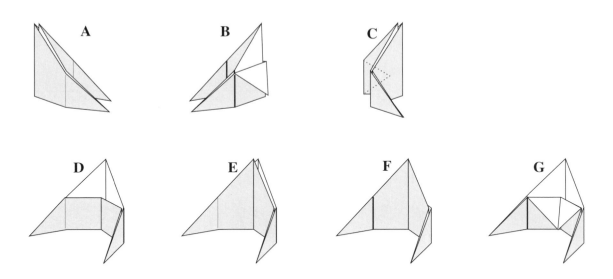

Answer: Correct bills are **A** and **E**. **E** is a bit opened **A**. Correct semi-bill is **F**. **F** looks like **E**, but it has a pocket on the back. All the other models are incorrect. **B** was folded backward in step ❹ on the previous page. **C** was folded backward in step ③ on page 2. The bottom of **C** looks like a letter **W** as shown in **I** below. The correct bottom is **H**. **D** and **G** have pockets inside.

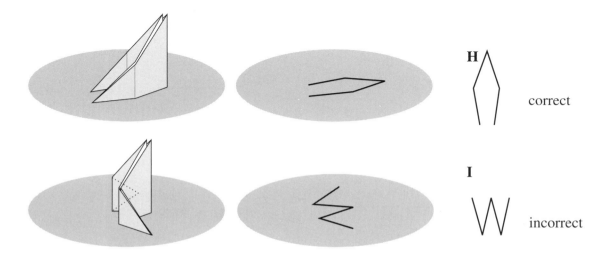

HAND MODULE (Bill + Semi-bill)

Interlock the bill and semi-bill. Don't make errors like 1 and **2** below.

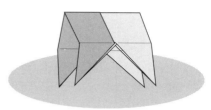

---

①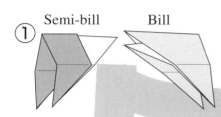
Semi-bill   Bill

The bill pinches the white part of the semi-bill.

②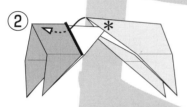

Insert the top ✳ between the space of the bold line.

③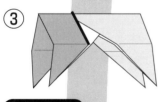

Completed

HAND MODULE

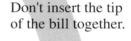

Error 1 ——— Error 2

It is wrong to let the tip ✳ of the bill cover the semi-bill.

Don't insert the tip of the bill together.

❸ 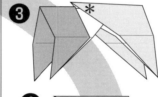   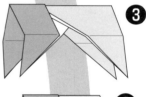 ❸

❹ 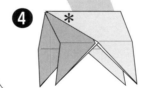   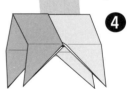 ❹

Semi-bill (It covers the bill.)

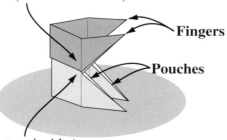

Fingers

Pouches

Bill (It stays inside.)

The four corners of the hand module have small bags. The tips of the bill are called **'pouch'** and the tips of the semi-bill **'finger'**. When making Basic Module A with two hand modules, insert the fingers into the pouches.

CONSTRUCTION OF BASIC MODULE A (Hand modules×2)

Make Basic Module A with two hand modules. Be sure to insert fingers (tips of the semi-bill) into pouches (tips of the bill).

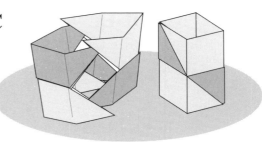

Insert **fingers** into **pouches**. ①

BASIC MODULE A

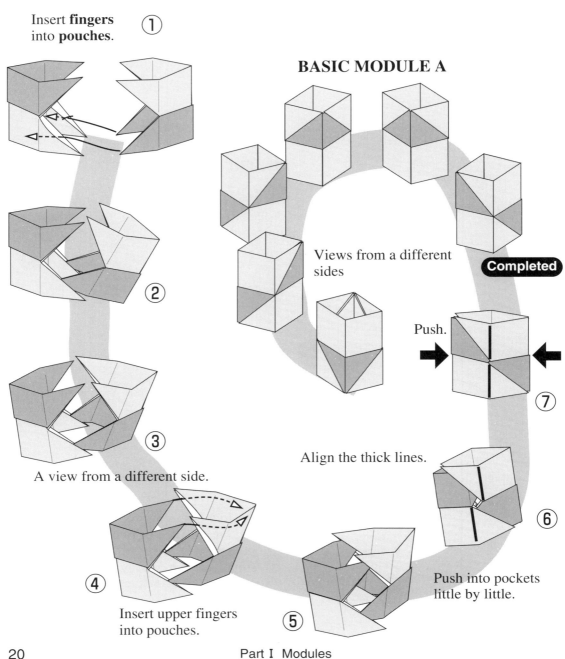

Views from a different sides

Completed

Push. ⑦

Align the thick lines. ⑥

②

③

A view from a different side.

④

Insert upper fingers into pouches.

⑤

Push into pockets little by little.

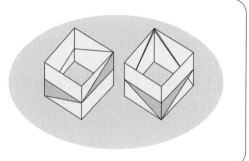

CHECKING

Look in at the completed module. If assembled correctly according to the directions, the inside will be yellow. If red sides appear, something is wrong. Try again from the start carefully with errors 1 and 2 on page 5 in mind.

WHEN YOU CANNOT ASSEMBLE CORRECTLY

Don't assemble in midair as shown on the previous page. Place your hands on the table, and insert the fingers carefully one by one.

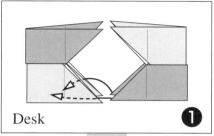

Desk ❶

Do the same as step ① on the previous page.

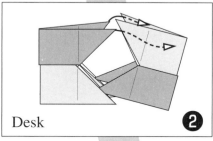

Desk ❷

Do the same as step ④ on the previous page.

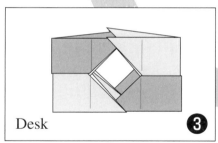

Desk ❸

Do the same as step ⑤ on the previous page.

Completed

When the thick lines are aligned, push both sides as indicated by arrows to make a square tube.

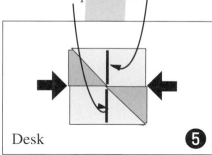

Desk ❺

Do the same as step ⑦ on the previous page.

Make sure that the thick lines are aligned. If they are not aligned, insert the fingers deeper.

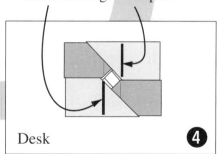

Desk ❹

Do the same as step ⑥ on the previous page.

ANOTHER TRY

Try to make the following Cylinder Module C ①-⑰ and try Basic Module A once again.

CYLINDER MODULE C (P2×4)

Make a **flat bill** and a **flat semi-bill** in place of a bill and a semi-bill.

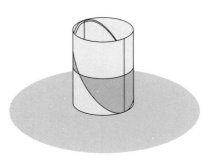

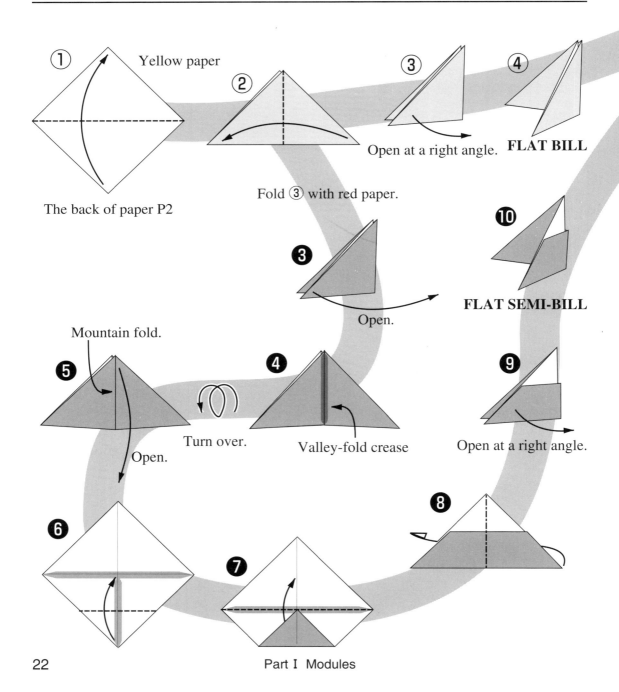

① Yellow paper

The back of paper P2

②

③ Open at a right angle. **FLAT BILL**

④

Fold ③ with red paper.

❸ Open.

❿ **FLAT SEMI-BILL**

❹ Valley-fold crease

Turn over.

❺ Mountain fold.

Open.

❾ Open at a right angle.

❻

❼

❽

CONSTRUCTION OF CYLINDER MODULE C

Fold ⑩-⑭ on the table.

FLAT SEMI-BILL **FLAT BILL**

⑤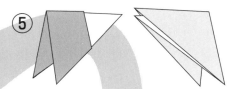

⑥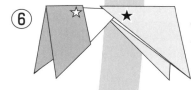

The flat bill pinches the flat semi-bill.

⑦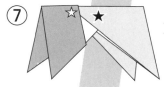

Insert ★ under ☆.

⑧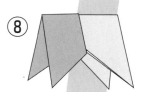

Make flat.

⑨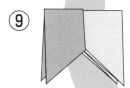

Follow steps ⑩-⑭ on the table.

⑩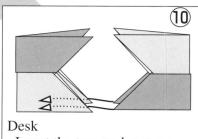

Desk
— Insert the two under corners. —

⑭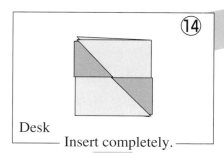

Desk
—— Insert completely. ——

⑬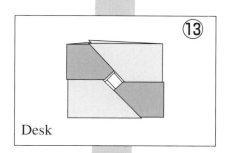

Desk

⑫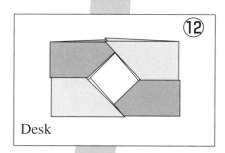

Desk

⑪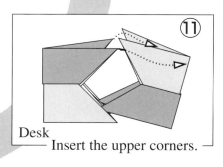

Desk
—— Insert the upper corners. ——

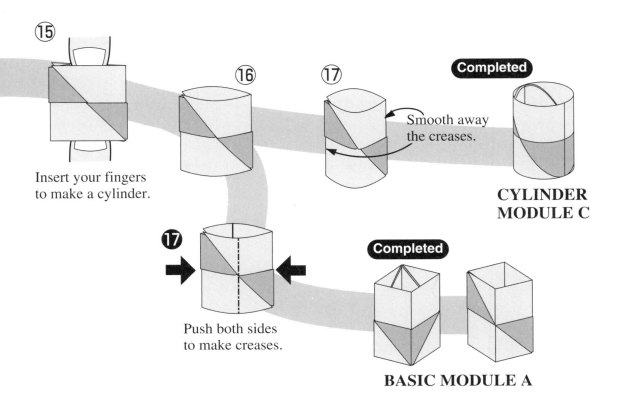

⑮

Insert your fingers
to make a cylinder.

⑯

⑰

Smooth away
the creases.

Completed

**CYLINDER
MODULE C**

⑰

Push both sides
to make creases.

Completed

BASIC MODULE A

— OUTSIDE POCKETS AND INSIDE POCKETS —

The dark parts in the right illustration are
called **pockets**. They are used for assembling
Basic Module A. When the modules are
completed, make sure that they have pockets.
If they look different from the illustrations
below, something is wrong. Try again
carefully, inserting fingers into pockets as on
page 6.

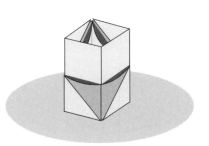

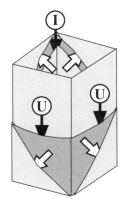

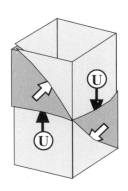

Ⓤ➡ Outside pockets

Ⓘ➡ Inside pockets

The pockets indicated by ⇨ are
not used for assembling modules.

SIMPLE MODULE B (Bill×4)

It is possible to make modules with only bills without using semi-bills. This model is similar to, but a little different from, one worked out by Isamu Asahi and Seiji Nishikawa.

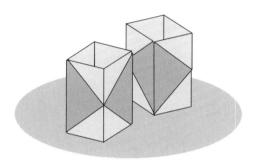

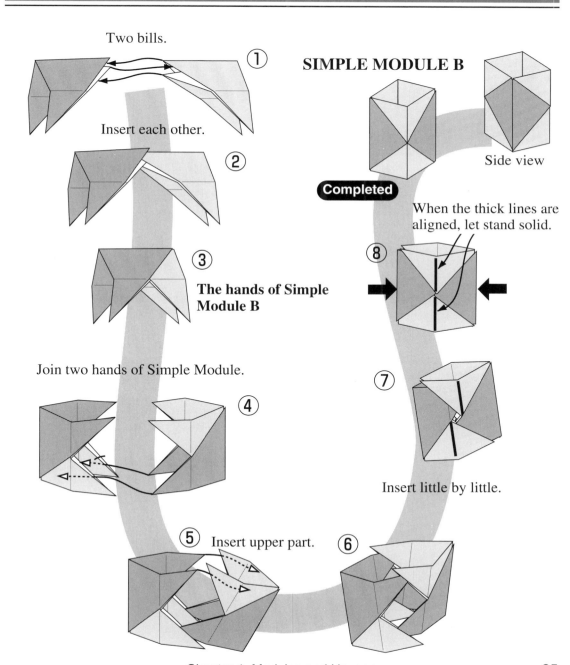

Two bills.

① Insert each other.

②

③ **The hands of Simple Module B**

Join two hands of Simple Module.

④

⑤ Insert upper part.

⑥

SIMPLE MODULE B

Side view

Completed

⑧ When the thick lines are aligned, let stand solid.

⑦

Insert little by little.

Problem 1-2 Make Basic Module A's, varying arrangements of colors of bills and semi-bills.

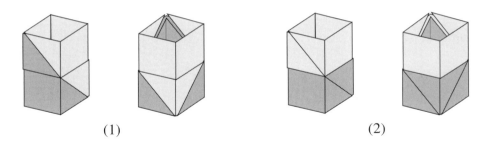

(1)   (2)

Problem 1-3 Make Simple Module B's varying arrangements of colors of bills.

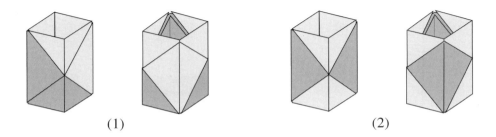

(1)   (2)

Problem 1-4 What module can you make, if you insert the fingers of hand (tips of semi-bill) into the pockets (tips of bill) as shown in (1) ? (2) is a correct assembly of Basic Module A.

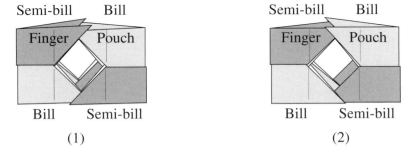

(1)   (2)

Answer to Problem 1-2(1) Join the bill and semi-bill of the same color to make hands like ① and ❶ and then assemble them like ③.

Answer to Problem 1-2(2) The color of the bill and semi-bill of ① and ❶ is contrary.

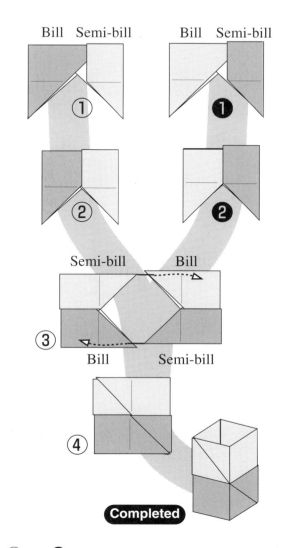

Bill   Semi-bill   Bill   Semi-bill

①   ❶

②   ❷

Semi-bill   Bill

③

Bill   Semi-bill

④

Completed

Answer to Problem 1-3 Change the semi-bill ① and ❶ in Problem 1-2 to the bill. The color arrangements are the same.

Answer to Problem 1-4 If you insert the pouches into the fingers, the parts ★ turn over like ③ and ④ and the result is incorrect.

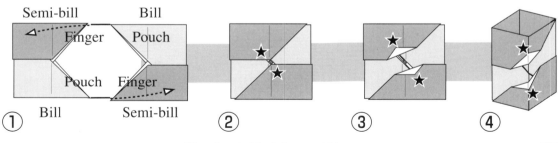

Semi-bill   Bill
Finger   Pouch

Pouch   Finger

① Bill   Semi-bill   ②   ③   ④

KITE MODULE K (P2×4)

You can make modules, using paper other than square paper. Presented here is Kite Module, which is made of kite-shape ②. You can also use rhombic paper. The method is the same as that of square paper.

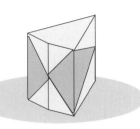

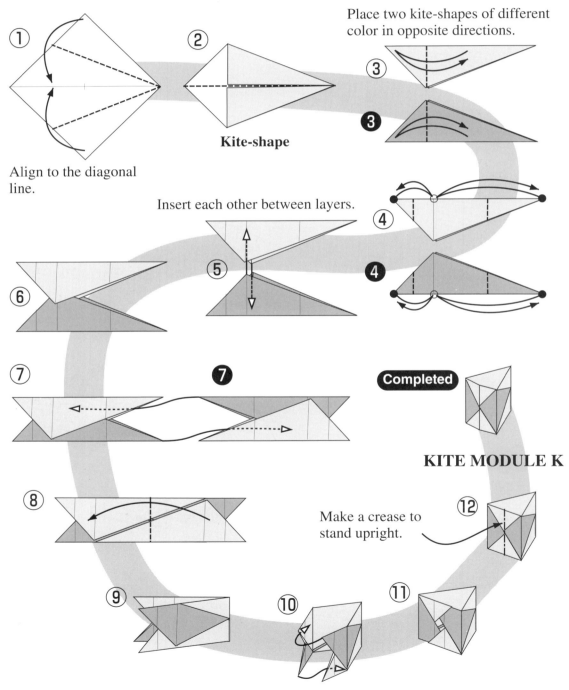

① Align to the diagonal line.

② **Kite-shape**

Place two kite-shapes of different color in opposite directions.

③

❸

Insert each other between layers.

④

❹

⑤

⑥

⑦

❼

⑧

Completed

KITE MODULE K

⑫ Make a crease to stand upright.

⑨

⑩

⑪

1.2

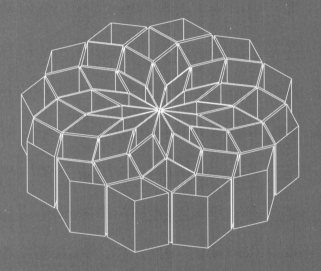

1.2 Blossoms
Short Joint S
S Side Assembly
Blossoms
Cherry Blossom
Chrysanthemum
Mass Production #1

SHORT JOINT S (P2)

Short Joint S (dark part in the right illustration) is used to join Basic Module A sideway. Use the same size of paper as the bill.

S SIDE ASSEMBLY

Insert both ends of **Short Joint S** into the outside pockets of Basic Module A's and join them.

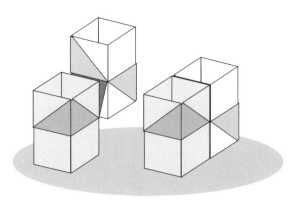

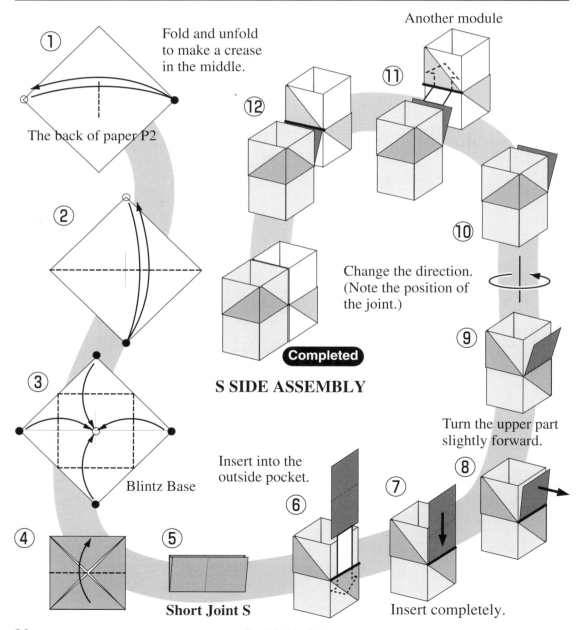

① Fold and unfold to make a crease in the middle.

The back of paper P2

②

③ Blintz Base

④

⑤ **Short Joint S**

⑥ Insert into the outside pocket.

⑦

⑧ Insert completely.

⑨ Turn the upper part slightly forward.

⑩ Change the direction. (Note the position of the joint.)

⑪ Another module

⑫

Completed

S SIDE ASSEMBLY

Practice 2-1 Make following models with Basic Module A's by means of S Side Assembly.

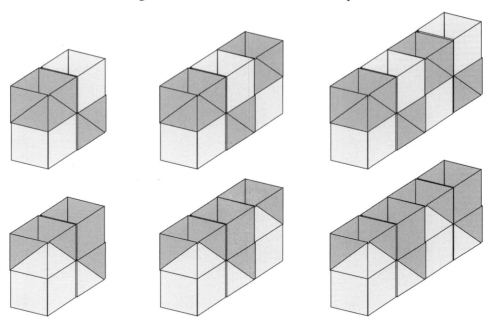

Problem 2-1 Which models used S Side Assembly? All the dark-colored modules face in the same direction.

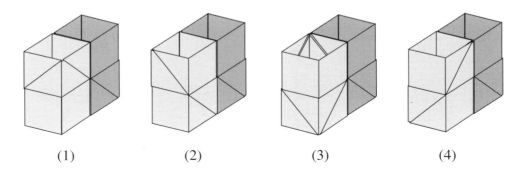

(1)   (2)   (3)   (4)

Answer (1) and (2). You cannot join the modules like (3) and (4), since the outside pockets, which come in contact, open downward. If you use Side Joint J on page 32, you can assemble the module like (3).

Practice 2-2 Join Basic Modules A's as below by means of S Side Assembly.

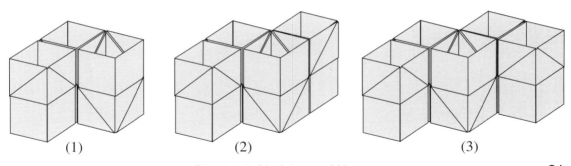

(1)   (2)   (3)

BASIC MODULE A VIEWD FROM ABOVE

If you see the modules from above, it is easy to understand the construction of **S Side Assembly of Basic Modules A's**. Each view of (1),(2),(3) of practice 2-3 from above looks like steps (1),(2) and (3) given below. The L marks in (4), (5) and (6) shows the direction of the **inside pockets**. The heavy lines in (7),(8) and (9) show **Short Joint S's**. In these illustrations, however, you cannot see the colors of bills and semi-bills.

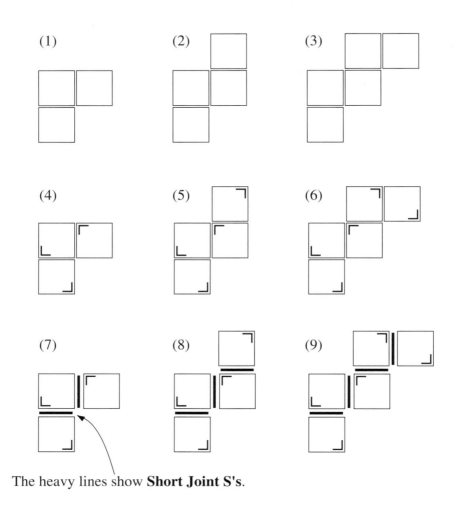

The heavy lines show **Short Joint S's**.

Practice 2-3 Execute S Side Assembly as below.

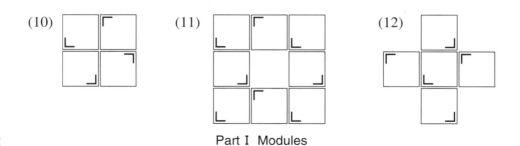

Part I Modules

BLOSSOM (P3×Petals×5)

Squash Basic Module A's a little and joint them by **S Side Assembly** to make a thick blossom.

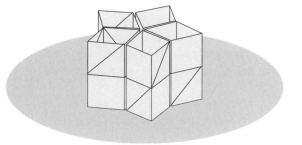

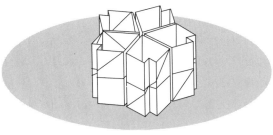

CHERRY BLOSSOM
(P3×25＝A×5+S×5)

Indent the corners of Basic Module A's to make petals. Join the five modules by **S Side Assembly** to make a cherry blossom. Indent one of the corners of ● shown in ① and ② below.

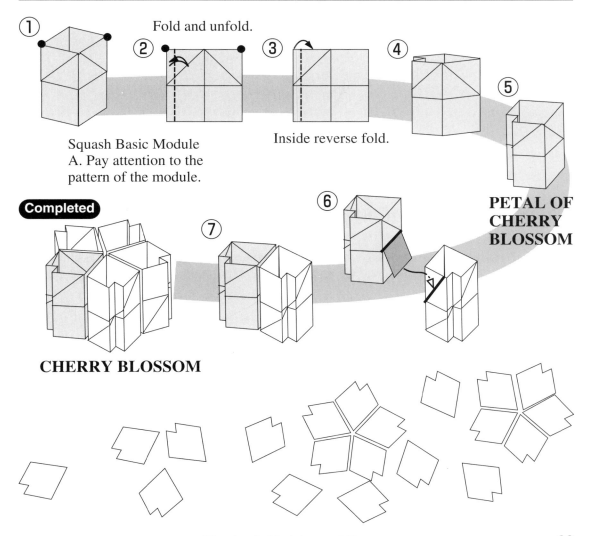

① ② Fold and unfold. ③ ④ ⑤

Squash Basic Module A. Pay attention to the pattern of the module.

Inside reverse fold.

PETAL OF CHERRY BLOSSOM

Completed

⑦ ⑥

CHERRY BLOSSOM

CHRYSANTHEMUM (Lots of P3)

You will need a lot of petals to make this
chrysanthemum. Divide paper P3 (6"/15 cm square)
into quarters. (See page 36 for details.)

CHRYSANTHEMUM FLOWERS (Lots of P3)

The center of (1) and (2) is made up of 8 modules and (3) of 12 modules. If you join
additional modules to each, you can make (4), (5) and (6). All the modules are assembled
methodically, and no diagrams will be necessary. If you use a variety of colorful paper, they
will look like fireworks.

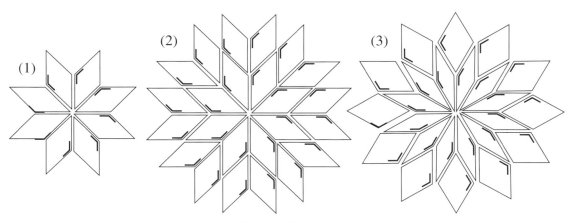

(1)

(2)

(3)

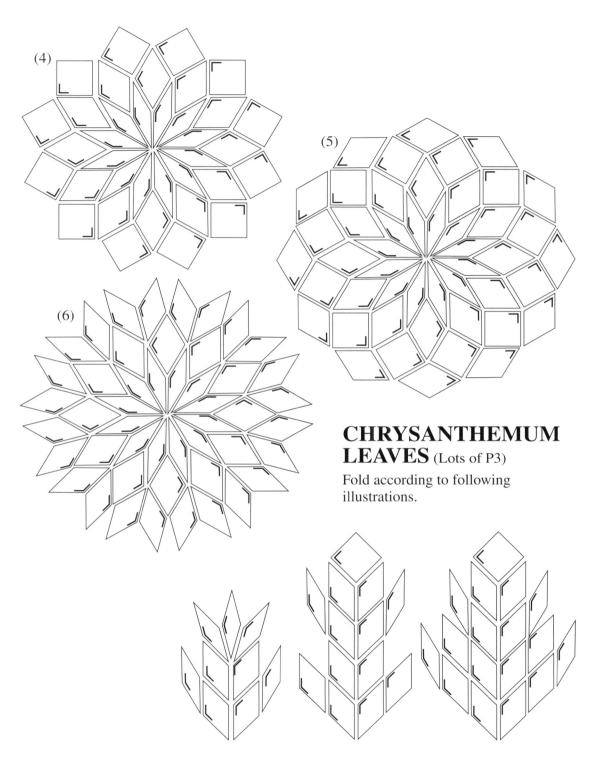

(4)

(5)

(6)

CHRYSANTHEMUM LEAVES (Lots of P3)

Fold according to following illustrations.

Problem 2-4 In making (1)-(6), how many Basic Module A's and Short Joint S's are used? How many pieces of paper are used?

Answer (A, S, Paper) → (8, 8, 40), (24, 32, 128), (24, 36, 132), (36, 60, 204), (48, 84, 276), (48, 72, 264).

MASS PRODUCTION 1 (P1)

In makeing models like the chrysanthemum, you have to prepare a lot of small modules and joints. In that case, cut the large paper into small pieces after creasing instead of preparing lots of small paper. The following is a method of making 16 bills or semi-bills from one ordinary paper.

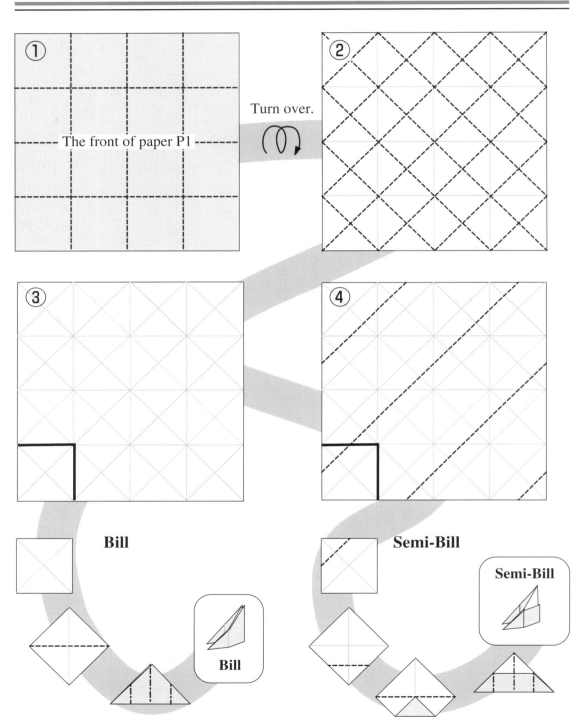

① The front of paper P1

Turn over.

②

③

④

Bill

Semi-Bill

Bill

Semi-Bill

1.3

1.3 Pile Construction
Pile Joint T
Long Joint L
Pile Construction of Basic Module A
Pile Construction of Kite Module K

PILE JOINT T (P2)

A component which is to assemble Basic Module A's vertically.

LONG JOINT L (P2)

Long Joint L is step ⑤ of the following **Pile Joint T**. It is used to assemble modules horizontally.

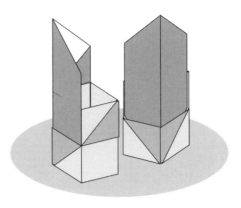

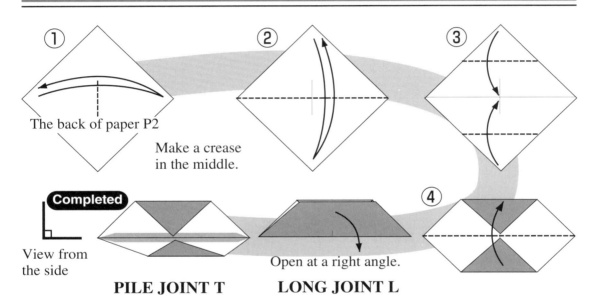

The back of paper P2

Make a crease in the middle.

Completed

View from the side

PILE JOINT T

Open at a right angle.

LONG JOINT L

OUTSIDE INSERTION OF PILE JOINT T

Open Pile Joint T at a right angle and insert into the outside pockets of the module along the long sides.

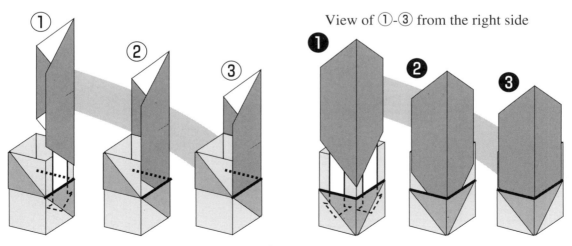

View of ①-③ from the right side

INSIDE INSERTION OF PILE JOINT T

Insert the Pile Joint T into the inside pockets of the module.

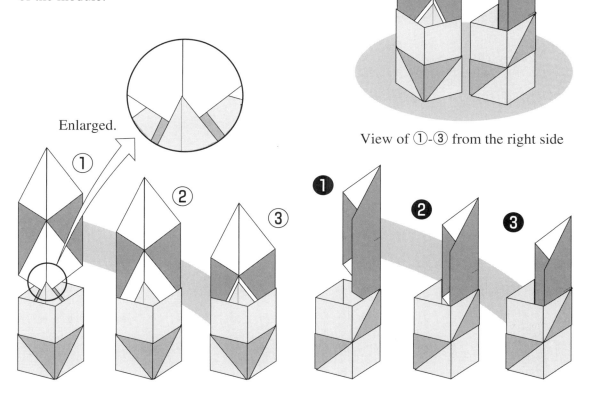

Enlarged.

View of ①-③ from the right side

THE RELATION BETWEEN OUTSIDE AND INSIDE INSERTIONS

Pile Joint T looks like a letter L from above. It is possible to insert it into the outside or inside pocket as shown below.

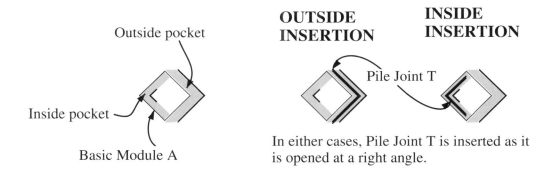

Outside pocket

Inside pocket

Basic Module A

OUTSIDE INSERTION

INSIDE INSERTION

Pile Joint T

In either cases, Pile Joint T is inserted as it is opened at a right angle.

Problem 3-1 Select the correct Outside Insertion of Pile Joint T's from (1)-(4).

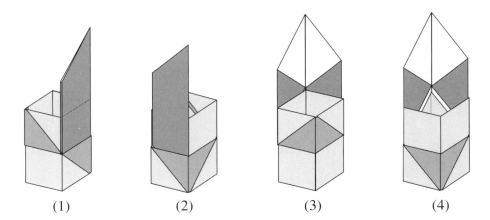

(1)　　　　　　(2)　　　　　　(3)　　　　　　(4)

Answer Only (3) is correct. The joint is inserted into the outside pockets of the other side. In (1) and (2), Long Joint L's are inserted in place of Pile Joint T's. (4) is Inside Insertion.

Problem 3-2 Select the correct Inside Insertion of Pile Joint T's from (1)-(5).

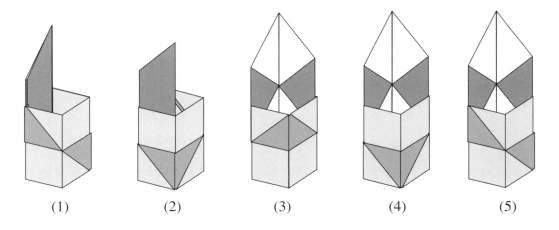

(1)　　　　(2)　　　　(3)　　　　(4)　　　　(5)

Answer All models are wrong. (1) and (2) are Long Joint L's. (3) and (5) look correct, but the joints are not inserted into the inside pockets. Compare them with (4) in Practice 3-1, and see the difference. In the right models Pile Joint T's are inserted deeper and stick out of the other side. They do not function as joints.

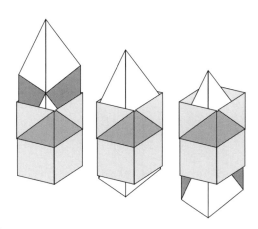

PILE CONSTRUCTION OF
BASIC MODULE A (A×2+T×2)

Using two Pile Joint T's, you can assemble
Basic Module A's vertically. In this case, one
end of Pile Joint T is inserted into inside
pockets and the other into outside pockets.
Don't forget this rule.

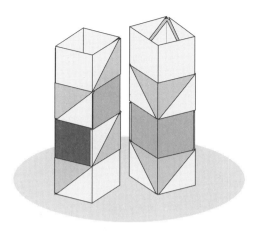

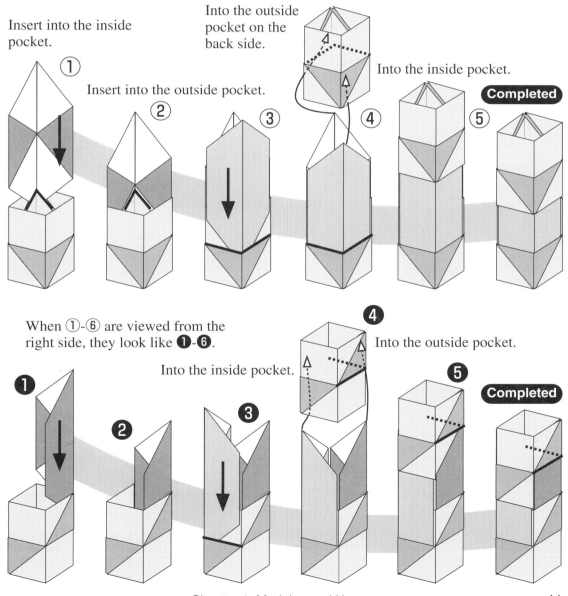

Insert into the inside pocket.

① Insert into the outside pocket.

② Into the outside pocket on the back side.

③ Into the inside pocket.

④ ⑤ **Completed**

When ①-⑥ are viewed from the right side, they look like ❶-❻.

❶ Into the inside pocket. ❷ ❸ ❹ Into the outside pocket. ❺ **Completed**

Problem 3-3 Make the following patterns by assembling Basic Module A's and Simple Module B's.

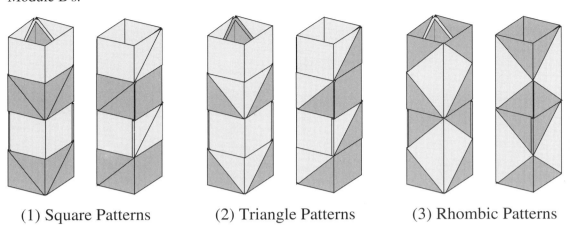

(1) Square Patterns   (2) Triangle Patterns   (3) Rhombic Patterns

Answer The square patterns are made up of Basic Module A's in Practice 1-2(2) on page 12. The triangle patterns are made up of Basic Module A's in Practice 1-2(1). The rhombic patterns are assembled with Simple Module B's in Practice 1-3(2) as follows.
The inside color of Pile Joint T has nothing to do with patterns, since it is hidden behind the module, but the outside color affects the patterns, since it appears on the surface.
Make a variety of patterns freely, keeping the above point in mind.

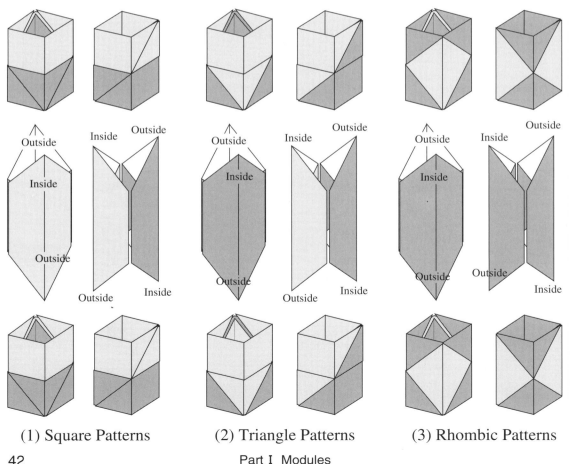

(1) Square Patterns   (2) Triangle Patterns   (3) Rhombic Patterns

Problem 3-4 If both ends of Pile Joint T (dark part) are inserted into the inside pockets or outside pockets, what will happen?

Problem 3-5 Join the Pile Construction of Basic Module A's horizontally, using Long Joint L. Hint: S Side Assembly.

Answer to Problem 3-4 If both ends of Pile Joint T are inserted into the inside pockets, the whole will be hidden like (1). If inserted into the outside pockets, most of the part will appear on the surface like (2). ((3) is the view from the left). It is not a good assembly, though possibly, since the Pile Joint T turns up like (4).

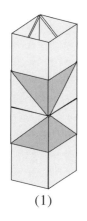

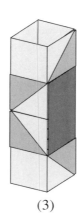

Turn up and unstable.

(1)   (2)   (3)   (4)

Answer to Problem 3-5 Insert both ends of Long Joint L into the joint (thick line of ① and ②) of Basic Module A's. When completed, it will disappear like S Side Assembly.

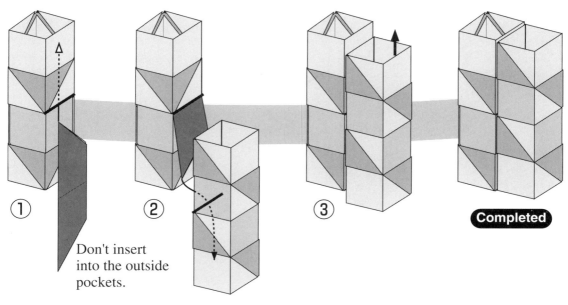

①   ②   ③   **Completed**

Don't insert into the outside pockets.

PILE CONSTRUCTION OF KITE MODULE K

(Kite-shape module×2＋P2×2)

Assembly in the same way as Pile Construction
of Basic Module A's with a non-symmetrical
pile joint.

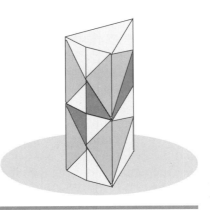

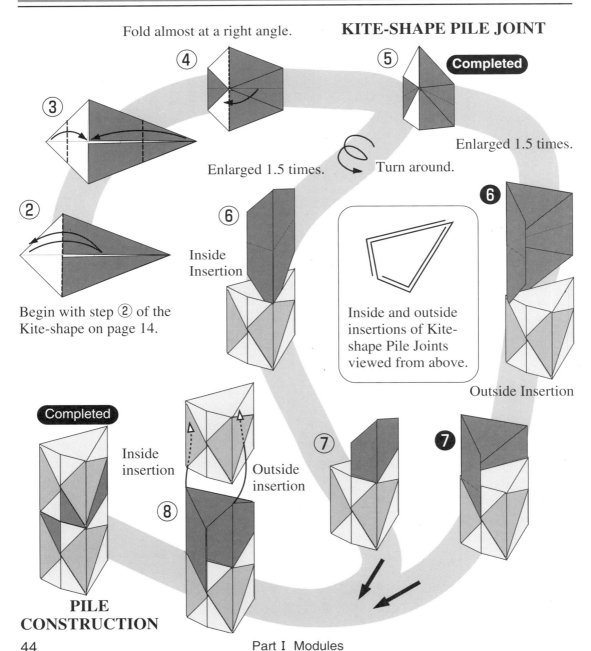

Fold almost at a right angle.

KITE-SHAPE PILE JOINT

④

⑤ Completed

③

Enlarged 1.5 times.

Enlarged 1.5 times. Turn around.

②

Begin with step ② of the
Kite-shape on page 14.

⑥ Inside
Insertion

⑥

Inside and outside
insertions of Kite-
shape Pile Joints
viewed from above.

Outside Insertion

Completed

Inside
insertion

Outside
insertion

⑦

❼

⑧

**PILE
CONSTRUCTION**

Part I Modules

1.4

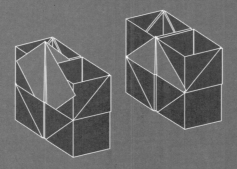

1.4 J Side Assembly

Side Joint J
J Side Assembly
J Side Assembly of Four Modules
Side Joint J4

SIDE JOINT J (P2)

The joint is used to assemble Basic
Module A's and Simple Module B's side
by side. The ★ in steps ①-⑦ shows the
center of paper.

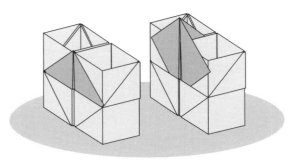

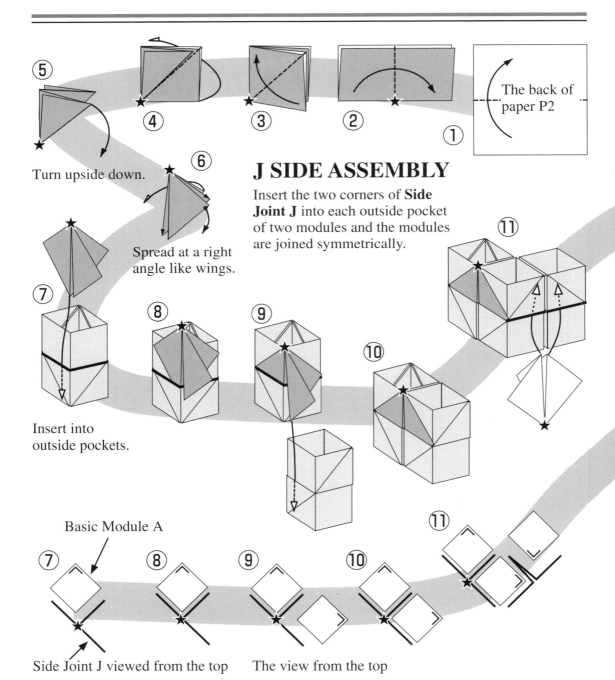

⑤

Turn upside down.

④

③

②

①

The back of
paper P2

⑥

Spread at a right
angle like wings.

J SIDE ASSEMBLY

Insert the two corners of **Side
Joint J** into each outside pocket
of two modules and the modules
are joined symmetrically.

⑦

Insert into
outside pockets.

⑧

⑨

⑩

⑪

Basic Module A

⑦

⑧

⑨

⑩

⑪

Side Joint J viewed from the top

The view from the top

Part I Modules

J SIDE ASSEMBLY OF
FOUR MODULES (A×4+J×4)

Four Basic Module A's are jointed together by the method of **J Side Assembly** with **Side Joint J's**. This cube forms the basis of the house introduced from page 35 onward.

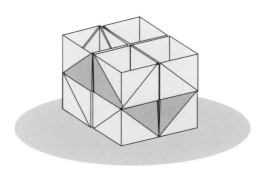

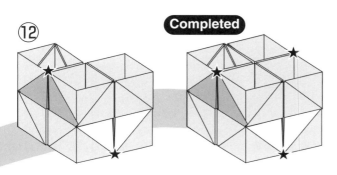

⑫ **Completed**

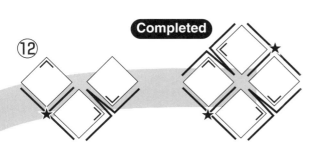

⑫ **Completed**

Problem 4-1 Carry out the following **J Side Assembly**. Enter thick lines showing the inside pockets of modules and Side Joint J's.

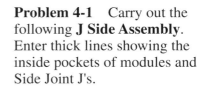

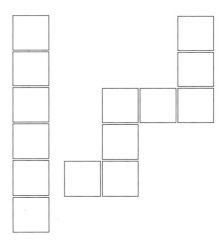

Answer to 4-1 The **M** and **N** are views of Side Joint J's from the top. **M** is the insertion from above like ⑦-⑩. **N** is the insertion from under like ⑪.

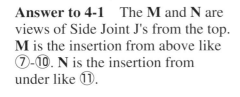

M   **N**

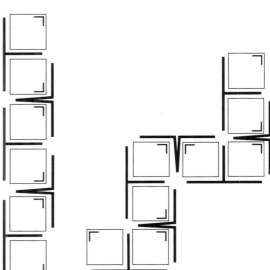

SIDE JOINT J4 (P2)

The joint makes it possible to assemble four modules together. The ★ is the center of paper.

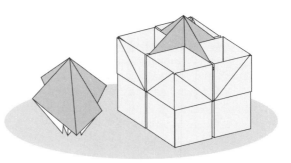

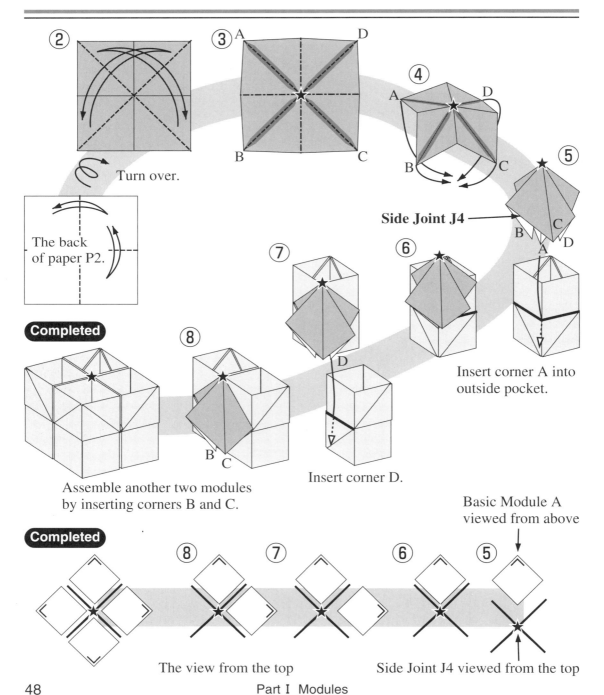

② Turn over.

③ A ... D / B ... C

The back of paper P2.

④ A / D / ★ / B / C

⑤ ★ / B / C / A / D

Side Joint J4

⑥

Insert corner A into outside pocket.

⑦ D

Insert corner D.

Completed

⑧ B C

Assemble another two modules by inserting corners B and C.

Basic Module A viewed from above

Completed

⑧ ⑦ ⑥ ⑤

The view from the top

Side Joint J4 viewed from the top

1.5

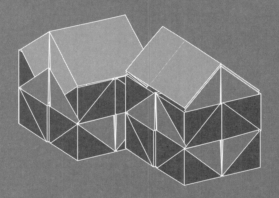

1.5 Small House

The Basis of Roof
Two Kinds of Small Houses
Long House 1
Long House 2
Twin-Roofed House
Tall House

THE BASIS OF ROOF (P1)

There are a variety of roofs depending on the size and shape of a house. First, let's master the basic construction of roof, which is applicable to all houses.

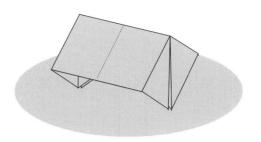

THE BASIS OF ROOF

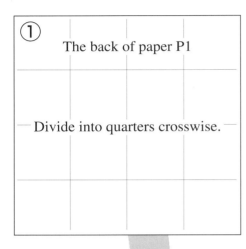

① The back of paper P1

Divide into quarters crosswise.

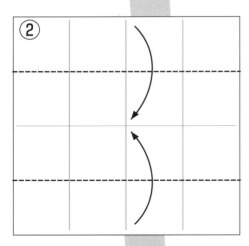

②

③

Completed

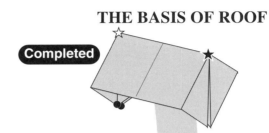

Make the same fold at ★.

⑦

The view from the other side

⑥

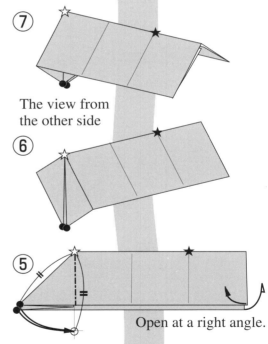

⑤ Open at a right angle.

Bring ● to ○ and make a mountain fold at a right angle.

④

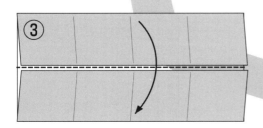

Inside reverse fold.

SHORT ROOF

(P1 or 6"/15 cm×5"/13 cm)

The Basis of Roof is too long for **a small house**. Adjust the length of paper as in ①-④. If you use paper of 6"/15 cm×5"/13 cm, you can skip steps ①-③ and fold it in the same way as the **Basis of Roof**.

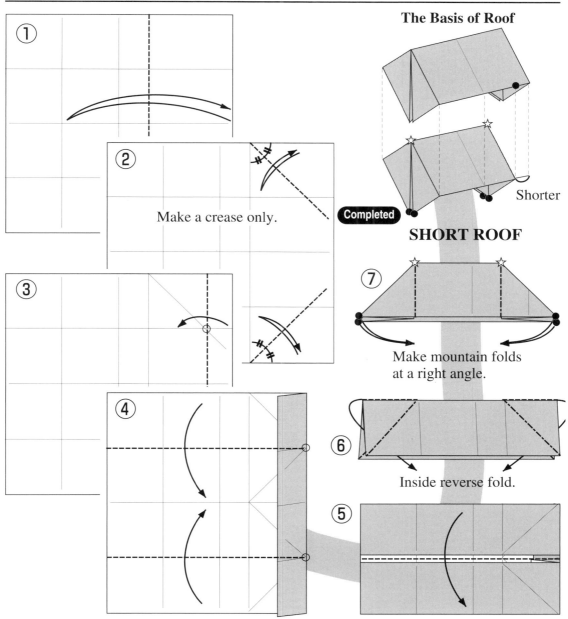

The Basis of Roof

Shorter

Completed

SHORT ROOF

①

② Make a crease only.

③

④

⑤

⑥ Inside reverse fold.

⑦ Make mountain folds at a right angle.

TWO KINDS OF SMALL HOUSES

(**A**×4+**J**×6+**Short Roof**)

The main body of a small house is made up of J Side Assembly of four Basic Module A's. If you put a short roof over this body, you can make a small house. There are two ways to inserting the roof, **outside and inside**.

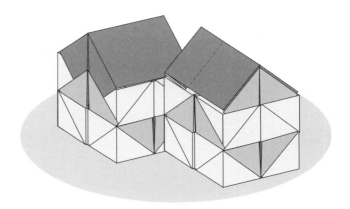

OUTSIDE INSERTION OF ROOF

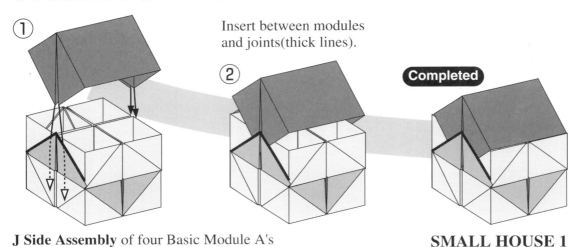

① Insert between modules and joints(thick lines).

②

Completed

J Side Assembly of four Basic Module A's

SMALL HOUSE 1

PRACTICE OF ROOFING

Side Joint J's

The roof sides have the same construction as Side Joint J's. If you find it difficult to fix the roof, practice with Side Joint J's.

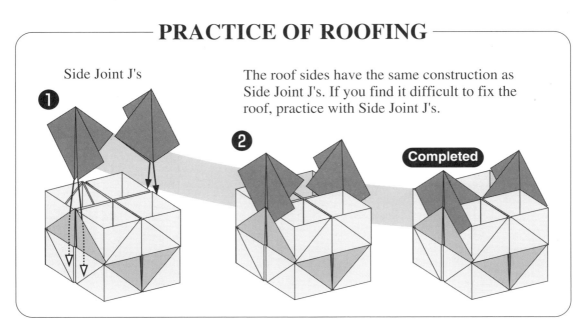

❶

❷

Completed

INSIDE INSERTION OF ROOF

First, insert Side Joint J's(①-③). To distinguish the joints from the body (wall), gray color is used in the diagrams, but you had better use the same color.

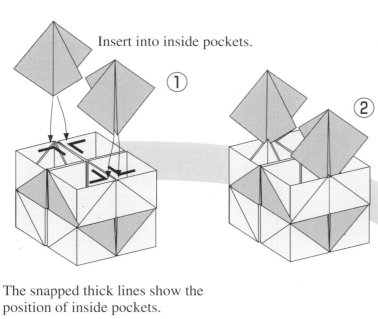

Insert into inside pockets.

The snapped thick lines show the position of inside pockets.

SMALL HOUSE 2

Completed

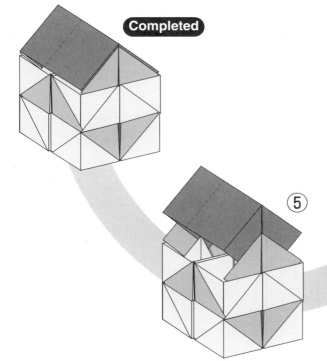

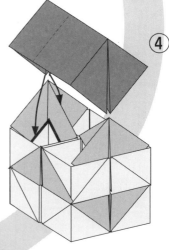

Insert the corners of the roof into the space shown by thick lines in the same way as in steps ①-③. Do the same for the corners in front.

LONG HOUSES 1

(A×8+J×6+S×4+**Long Roof**)

The body of **Long House 1** is made up of
the body of Small House, which is joined
with four Basic Module A's with Short Joint
S's. The roof is the one given on the
following page.

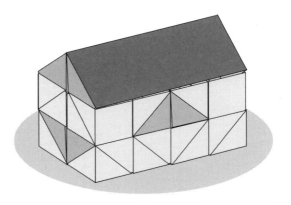

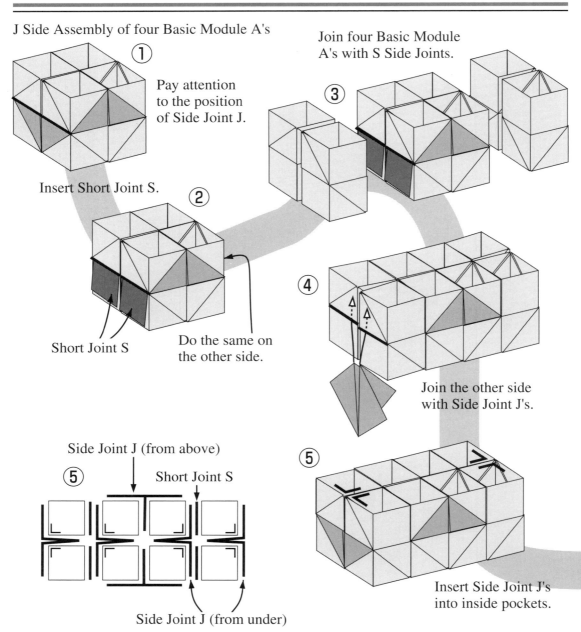

J Side Assembly of four Basic Module A's

① Pay attention
to the position
of Side Joint J.

Insert Short Joint S.

② Short Joint S

Do the same on
the other side.

Join four Basic Module
A's with S Side Joints.

③

④ Join the other side
with Side Joint J's.

Side Joint J (from above)

⑤ Short Joint S

Side Joint J (from under)

⑤ Insert Side Joint J's
into inside pockets.

LONG ROOF

Fold with paper 6"/15 cm×7³/8"/19 cm
in the same way as the **Basis of Roof**.

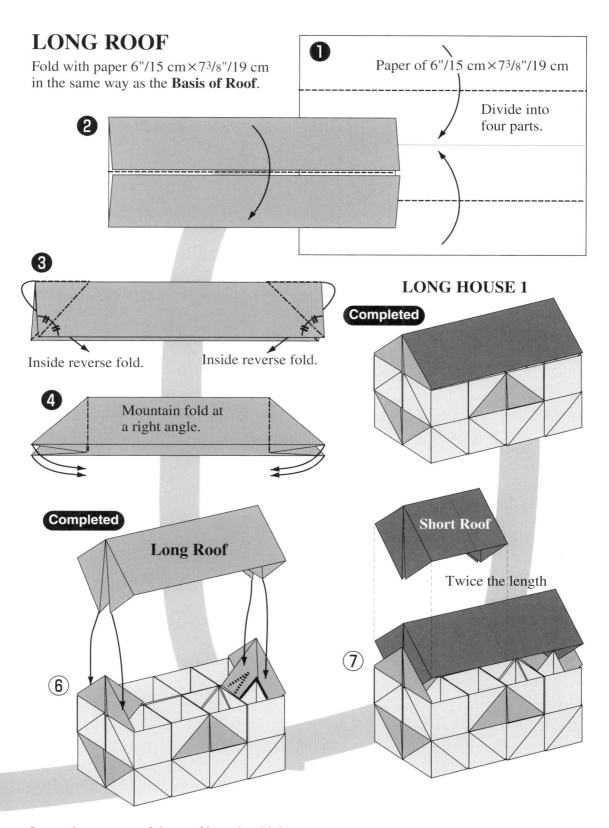

❶ Paper of 6"/15 cm×7³/8"/19 cm

Divide into
four parts.

❷

❸

Inside reverse fold.   Inside reverse fold.

❹ Mountain fold at
a right angle.

LONG HOUSE 1

Completed

Completed

Long Roof

Short Roof

Twice the length

⑥

⑦

Insert the corners of the roof into the thick
lines. Do the same on the left side.

LONG HOUSES 2
(A×8+J×6+J4+Long Roof)

The modules of the body are assembled
in a different way from that of **Long
House 1**.

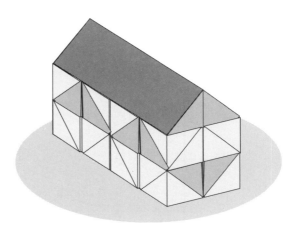

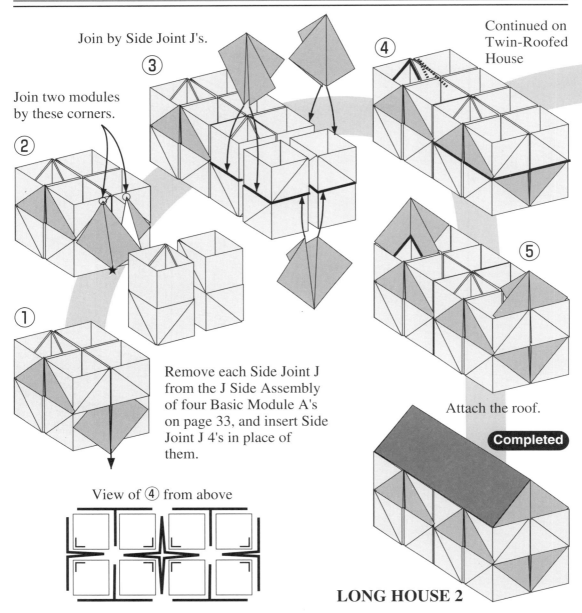

Join by Side Joint J's.

③

Join two modules
by these corners.

②

④

Continued on
Twin-Roofed
House

⑤

①

Remove each Side Joint J
from the J Side Assembly
of four Basic Module A's
on page 33, and insert Side
Joint J 4's in place of
them.

Attach the roof.

Completed

View of ④ from above

LONG HOUSE 2

TWIN-ROOFED HOUSE
(A×8+J×6+J4+Long Roof)
If you turn Long House 2 upside down, you
can fix two roofs as shown on the right.

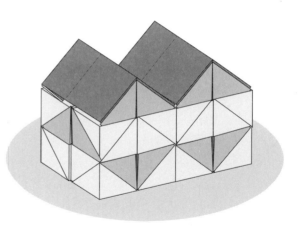

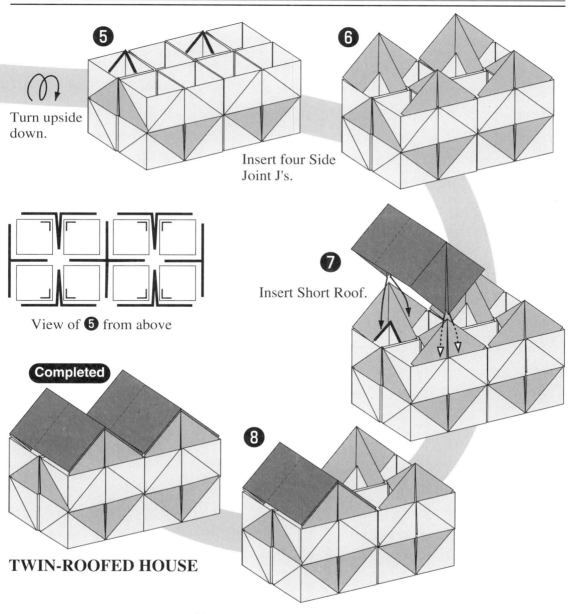

5

Turn upside
down.

Insert four Side
Joint J's.

View of **5** from above

6

7

Insert Short Roof.

8

Completed

TWIN-ROOFED HOUSE

TALL HOUSE
(A×8+J×10+Short Roof)

Join four piles of Basic Module A's
together and carry out J Side Assembly.
If you put a roof over them, you can
make a Tall House.

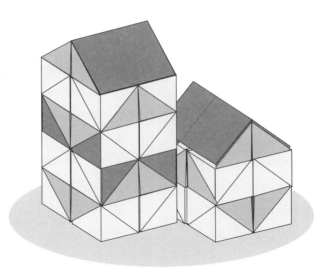

J Side Assembly with two
piles of Basic Module A's.

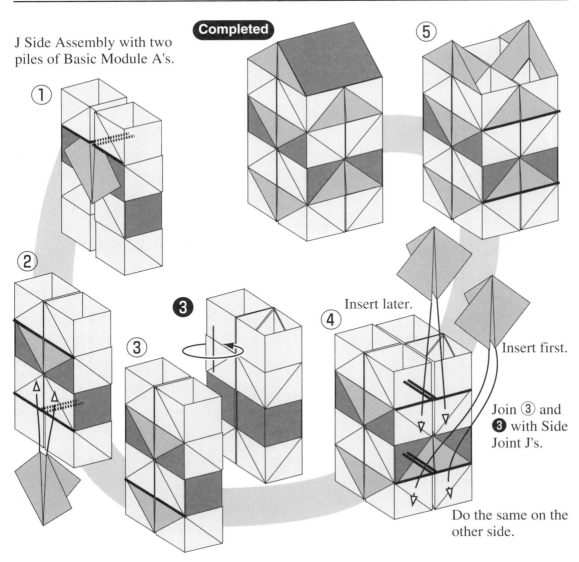

Completed

⑤

①

②

❸

③

④ Insert later.

Insert first.

Join ③ and
❸ with Side
Joint J's.

Do the same on the
other side.

58   Part I Modules

1.6

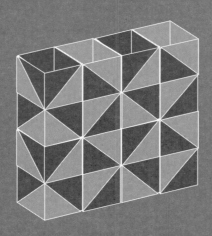

1.6 Lids and Nail
Natural Lid
Reverse Lid
Nail
Mass Production 2
Mass Production 3

NATURAL LID (P2)

Since the top and bottom of Basic Module A are open, it easily collapses when pressed from the sides. If you put a **lid** on it, the square top is fixed and it will not be deformed.

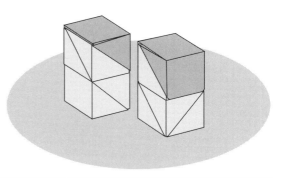

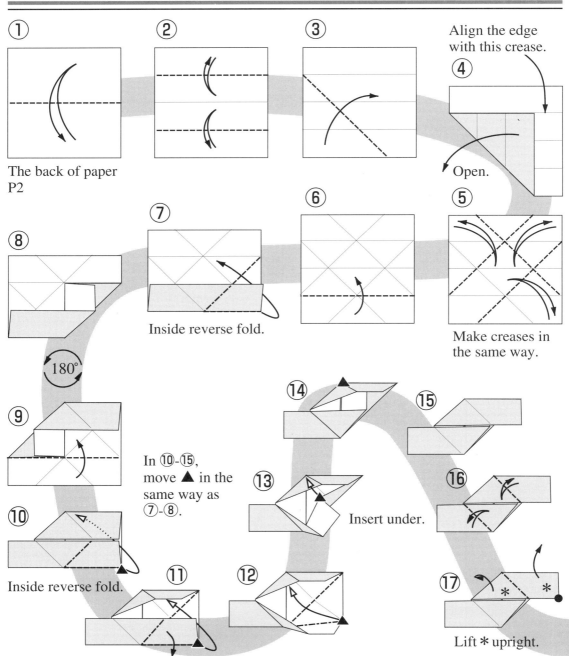

① The back of paper P2

②

③

Align the edge with this crease.

④ Open.

⑤ Make creases in the same way.

⑥

⑦ Inside reverse fold.

⑧

180°

⑨

In ⑩-⑮, move ▲ in the same way as ⑦-⑧.

⑩ Inside reverse fold.

⑪

⑫

⑬ Insert under.

⑭

⑮

⑯

⑰ Lift * upright.

60   Part I Modules

HOW TO FIX THE NATURAL LID

Insert each corner of natural lid, ● and ○ , into inside and outside pockets, respectively.

Insert each corner ○ to inside pocket.

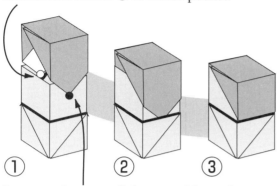

① ② ③

Insert each corner ● into outside pocket.

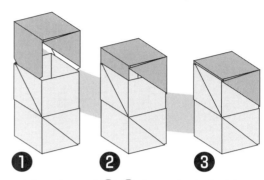

❶ ❷ ❸

The view of ①-③ from the left side

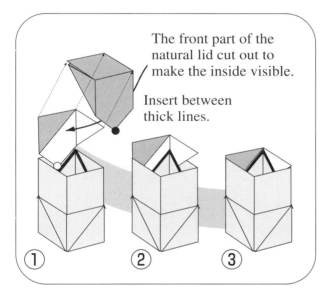

The front part of the natural lid cut out to make the inside visible.

Insert between thick lines.

① ② ③

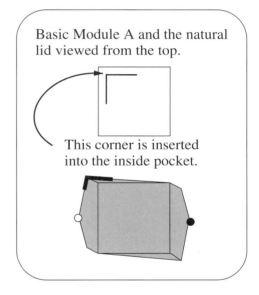

Basic Module A and the natural lid viewed from the top.

This corner is inserted into the inside pocket.

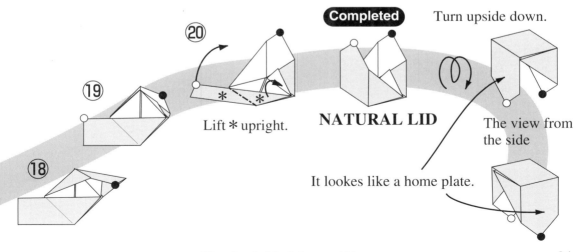

⑱

⑲

⑳

Lift * upright.

Completed Turn upside down.

NATURAL LID

The view from the side

It lookes like a home plate.

SMOOTH FOLDING OF NATURAL LID

Once you understand the construction of the natural lid, try the following easy way.

The back of ⑤ on page 46

Place ※ over ＊.

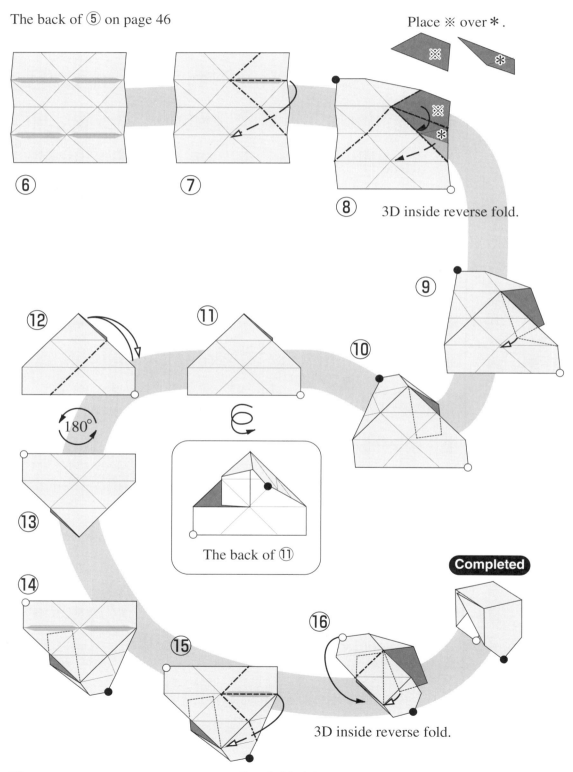

⑥

⑦

⑧ 3D inside reverse fold.

⑨

⑩

⑪

⑫

180°

⑬

The back of ⑪

Completed

⑭

⑮

⑯

3D inside reverse fold.

REVERSE LID (P2)

The lid folded in the opposite way, as if the natural lid is mirrored, is called a reverse lid. Parts of the process are omitted.

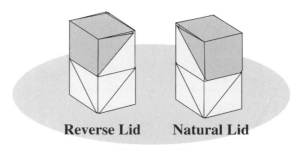

Reverse Lid **Natural Lid**

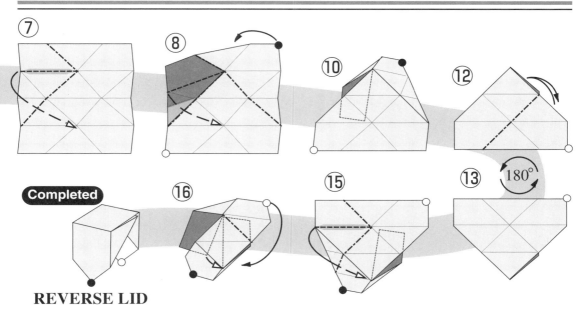

REVERSE LID

THE DIFFERENCE BETWEEN NATURAL AND REVERSE LIDS

The natural lid and reverse lid differ in the way of insertion.

The views of the left diagrams seen from the left

Natural lid

Reverse lid

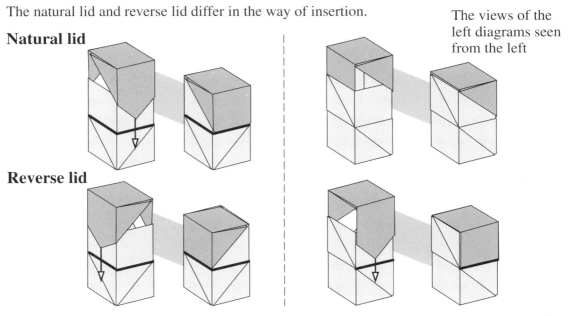

NAIL (P3)

P3 is a quarter of P2. The nail is used to fix the lid and it is also useful in forming patterns on the modules.

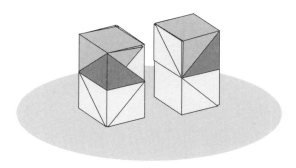

The back of paper P3

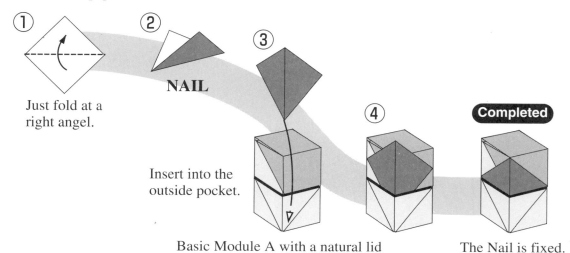

① Just fold at a right angel.

② NAIL

③ Insert into the outside pocket.

Basic Module A with a natural lid

④

Completed

The Nail is fixed.

USE OF NAIL 1

The lid is fixed firmly, since the area inserted is enlarged.

With the Nail   Without the Nail

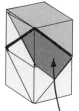

The area to be inserted is four times as larger.

The area inserted into the outside pocket.

USE OF NAIL 2

In making Bill, Semi-bill and Nail, if you use a variety of color paper, you can form attractive patterns as below.

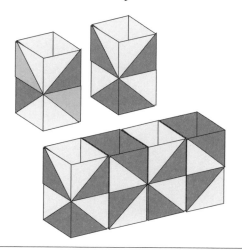

MASS PRODUCTION 2 (P1)

Mass-produce **Side Joint J, J4, Pile Joint T, Long Joint L, Hook Joint F** (p.96), and **Short Joint S.**

Begin with ② of **Mass Production 1** on page 22.

Begin with ④ of **Mass Production 1.**

3

5

For Side Joint J and J4

J4

J

For Long Joint L, Pile Joint T and Hook Joint F

T

L

F

Cut 5 1/8" off from top and left sides.

5 1/8" wide

5

5 1/8" wide

For Short Joint S

S

MASS PRODUCTION 3 (P1)

Mass-produce Lids and Nails.

Begin with ① of **Mass Production 1** on page 36.

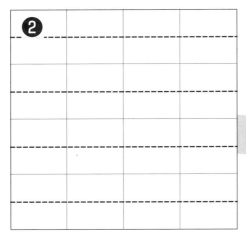

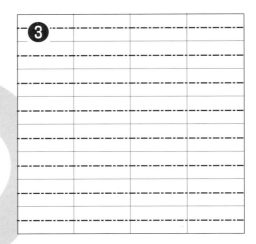

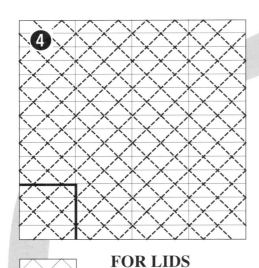

FOR LIDS

Begin with ❸ of **Mass Production 2**.

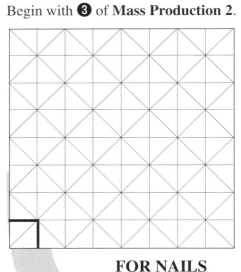

FOR NAILS

Lid

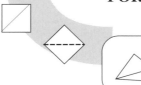

Nail

1.7

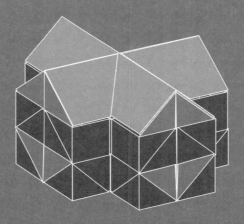

1.7 Cross House
**Cross House
Town Wall (Passage for Watchmen)
Small Tree**

CROSS HOUSE

(**A**×12+**J**×8+**J4**+S×8+**Long Roof**
+Overhang Roof×2)

Assemble four Basic Module A's with
Side Joint J's (p.48). Join eight Basic
Module A's with Short Joint S's to
make supports for **Overhang Roofs**.
Add a Long Roof and **Overhang
Roofs** (p.70).

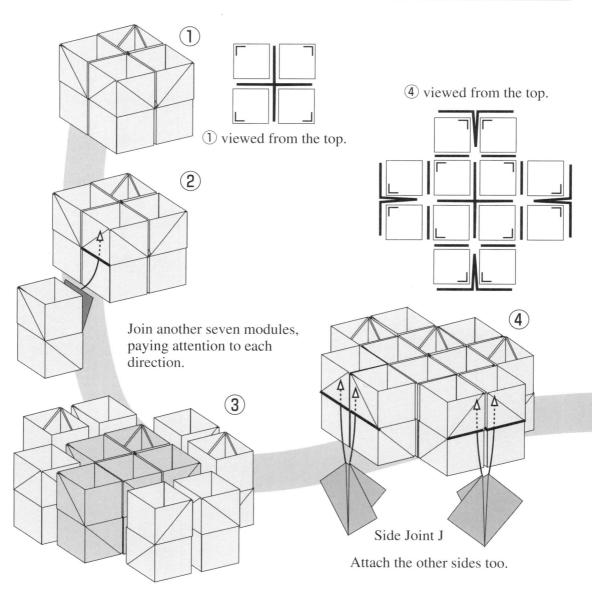

① viewed from the top.

④ viewed from the top.

Join another seven modules,
paying attention to each
direction.

Side Joint J

Attach the other sides too.

FIXING OF OVERHANG ROOFS

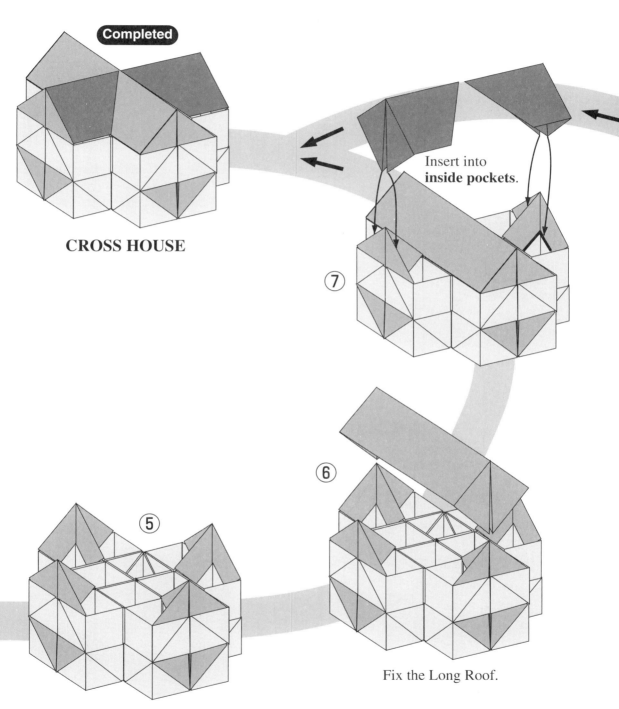

Completed

CROSS HOUSE

Insert into **inside pockets**.

⑦

⑥

Fix the Long Roof.

⑤

Complete the body of the **Cross House** by inserting four Side Joint J's from above.

OVERHANG ROOF

($3^{1}/_{2}$"/9.5 cm×6"/15 cm)

This roof projects over the modules. The structure is almost the same as that of a Short Roof.

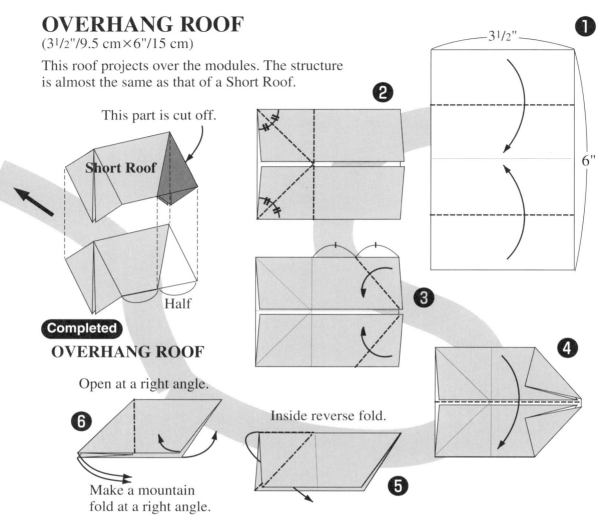

This part is cut off.

Short Roof

Completed

OVERHANG ROOF

Open at a right angle.

Inside reverse fold.

Half

Make a mountain fold at a right angle.

REINFORCEMENT OF OVERHANG ROOF

Put lids on Basic Module A's to fix the Overhang Roof firmly. Use a pair of a Natural Lid and a Reverse Lid.

R and **N** stand for Reverse Lid and Natural Lid respectively.

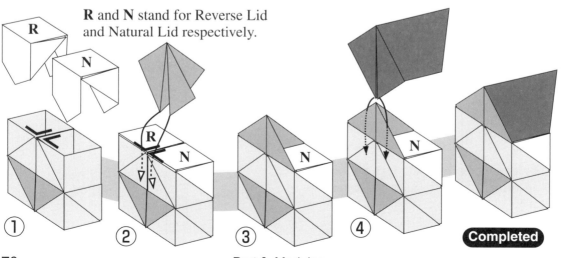

Completed

TOWN WALL (PASSAGE FOR WATCHMEN)

(⑤ of **Long House 1** (A×8+J×6+
S×4)+**Natural Lid**×4+**Reverse
Lid**×4+**Pillar**×4+**Long Roof**)

This is a wall found in an old town in
Europe. The street wall has a passage
or a room for watchmen. The lids
hidden in the Cross House turn out to
be the passage floor of the street wall.

PILLAR (P2)

The pillar supports the roof of the
street wall. Fold in a similar way as
Pile Joint T.

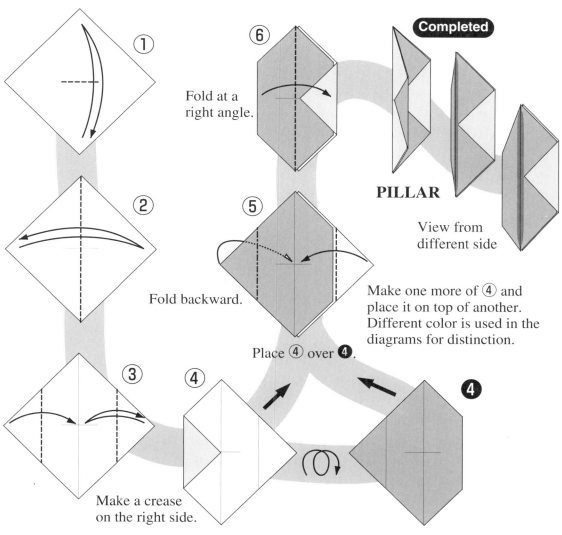

①

②

③ Make a crease
on the right side.

④

⑤ Fold backward.

Place ④ over ❹.

⑥ Fold at a
right angle.

Make one more of ④ and
place it on top of another.
Different color is used in the
diagrams for distinction.

Completed

PILLAR

View from
different side

CONSTRUCTION OF TOWN WALL

Put lids on ⑤ of Long House 1 on page 40
(① below) and then set up pillars. If you
tix a long roof to the house, then the town
wall is completed.

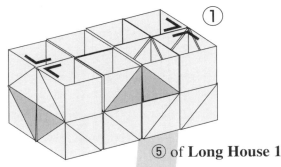

①

⑤ of **Long House 1**

Put lids on.

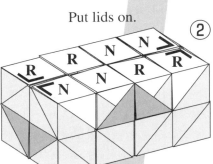

②

Insert pillars into inside pockets(marked ⌐).

A triangle appears
on the correct pillar.

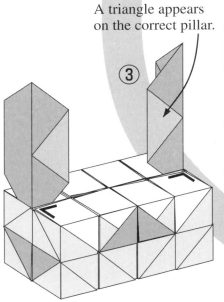

③

The wrong pillar

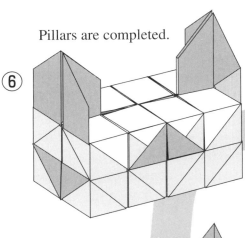

⑥

Pillars are completed.

⑤

Insert two more pillars.

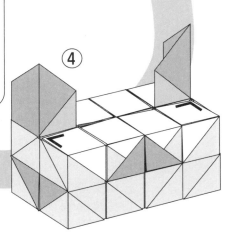

④

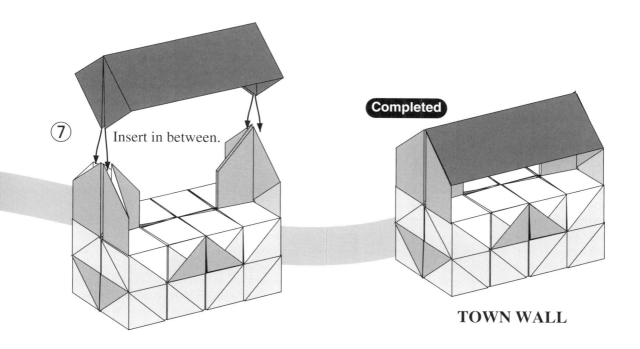

⑦ Insert in between.

Completed

TOWN WALL

If you find it difficult to fix the roof, follow the diagrams below.

PRACTICE OF FIXING THE ROOF TO PILLARS

Pillar are made up of two layers, so you can insert the corners of the roof between the layers. Since the structure of the corner of the roof and Side Joint J is the same, you can practice the process of insertion with Side Joint J.

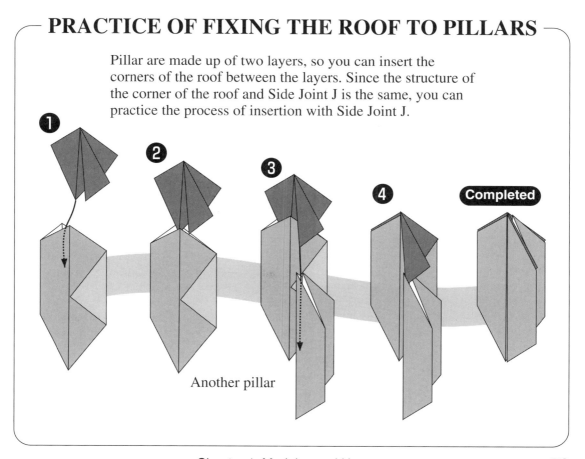

❶ ❷ ❸ ❹ **Completed**

Another pillar

SMALL TREE (Tsuda's Trunk + Branches)

This is a simple tree. Just insert branches into Yoshio Tsuda's trunk (next page).
(The folding of realistic trees are introduced in Tsuda's book, 'Creative Origami ' published by Ohtsuki Shoten.)

BRANCHES (About 4^{1}/$_{2}$"/12 cm square)

Just make an inside reverse fold at the corners of a **Preliminary Fold** to suit the shape of the tree.

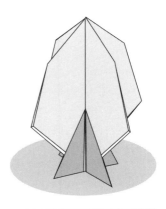

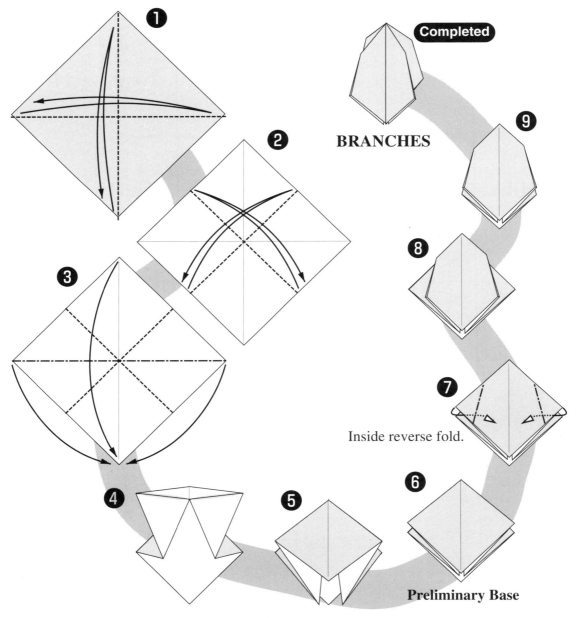

Completed

BRANCHES

❾

❽

❼ Inside reverse fold.

❻ **Preliminary Base**

❺

❹

❸

❷

❶

TSUDA'S TRUNK (About 3½"/9 cm square)

Only add one more fold to a bird base, which is used in the traditional crane fold. This trunk is superb.

STUMP (About 3½"/9 cm square)

Fold the top of Tsuda's trunk in half.

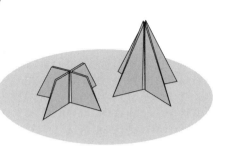

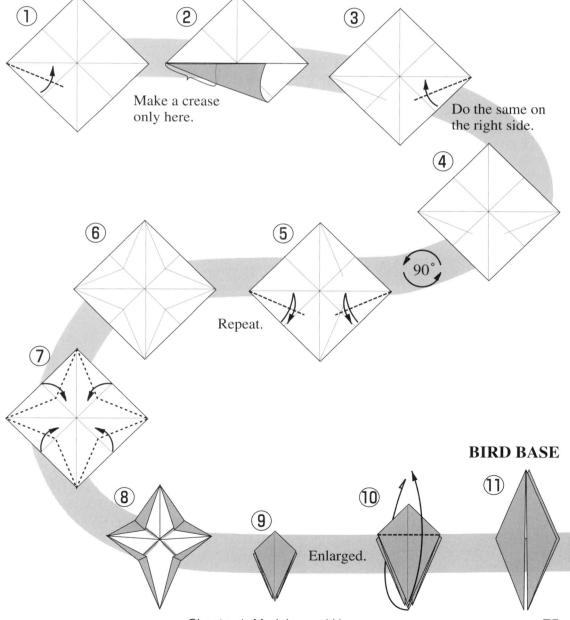

①

② Make a crease only here.

③ Do the same on the right side.

④

90°

⑤ Repeat.

⑥

⑦

⑧

⑨ Enlarged.

⑩

⑪

BIRD BASE

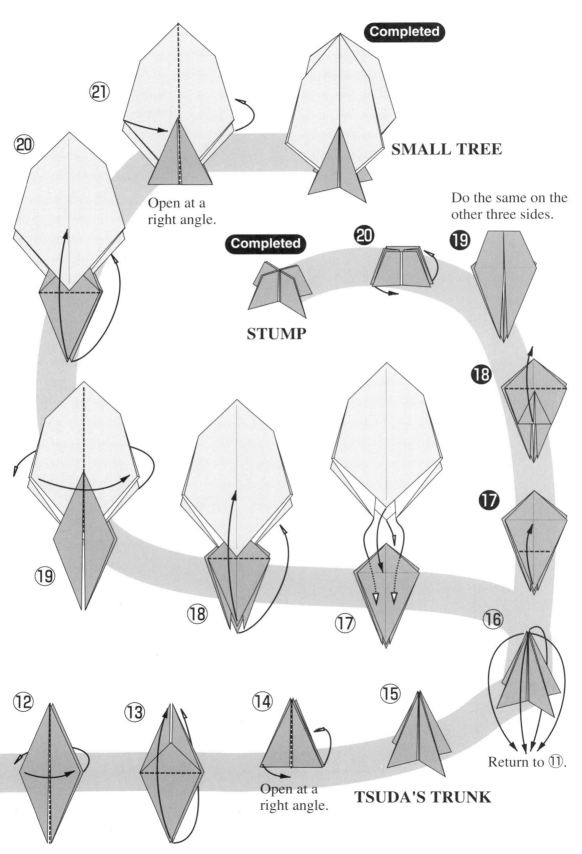

㉑

⑳ Open at a
right angle.

Completed

SMALL TREE

Do the same on the
other three sides.

Completed ⑳ ⑲

STUMP

⑱

⑲ ⑱ ⑰ ⑰

⑯

⑫ ⑬ ⑭ ⑮ Return to ⑪.

Open at a
right angle. **TSUDA'S TRUNK**

1.8

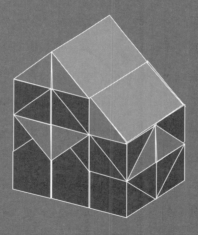

1.8 Large House
Foot
Long House with Foots
Large House

FOOT (P2×2)

Disassemble Basic Module A, and you can get the foot. If you fix the foots under the house, you can make a tall house.

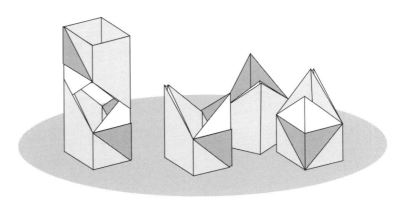

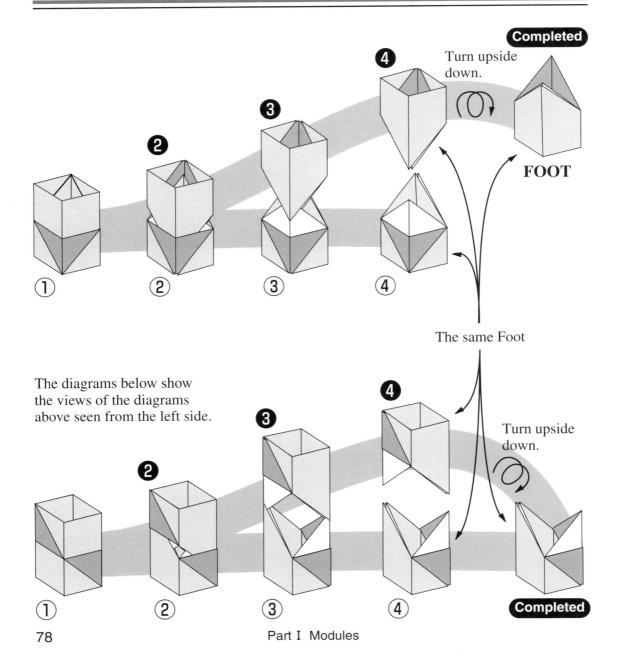

Completed

④ Turn upside down.

FOOT

❷ ❸ ❹

① ② ③ ④

The same Foot

The diagrams below show the views of the diagrams above seen from the left side.

❷ ❸ ❹

Turn upside down.

① ② ③ ④

Completed

HOW TO USE THE FOOT

The **foot** has two pointed tips. One is a tip of a single layer with the back of paper (white side) is shown. The other is tips of a double layer. Insert the tip of a single layer. Insert the tip of a single layer into the inside pocket of the module and sandwich the corner of the module with the tips of the double layer.

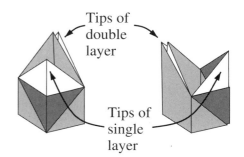

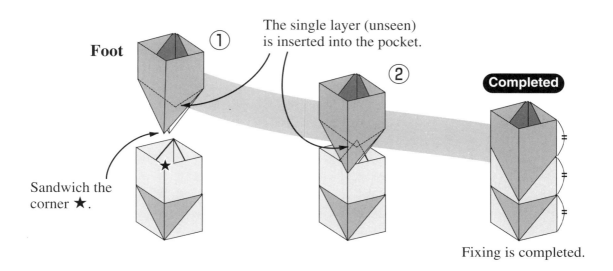

Foot

①

The single layer (unseen) is inserted into the pocket.

②

Completed

Sandwich the corner ★.

Fixing is completed.

❶ viewed from the left side.

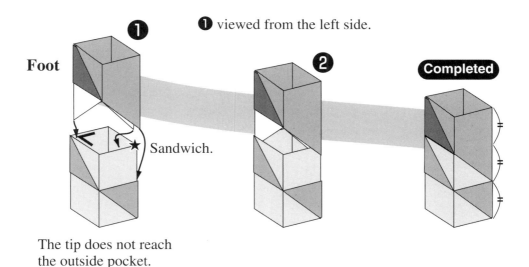

Foot

❶

❷

Completed

Sandwich.

The tip does not reach the outside pocket.

LONG HOUSE WITH FOOTS
(Long House 1 + Foot × 4)

Make the long house taller by adding
foots. The house illustrated below has
a roof to show which side is top, but
remove it when joining the foots. In
the example four foots are used, but
you may join more foots as desired.
The right diagram shows a house
with six foots and the opening satands
for an entrance.

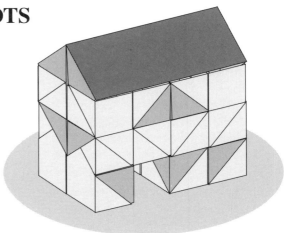

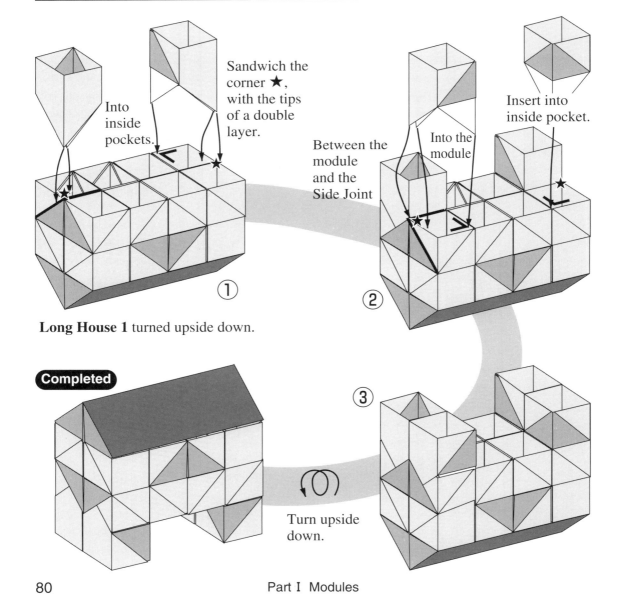

Into inside pockets.

Sandwich the corner ★, with the tips of a double layer.

Between the module and the Side Joint

Into the module

Insert into inside pocket.

① ② ③

Long House 1 turned upside down.

Completed

Turn upside down.

FASTENER OF FOOT (P2)

Side Joint J is useful in fastening feet. Diagrams ①-③ below show how to fix a fastener to **Long House 1**. The white triangle is the **Fastener of Feet**.

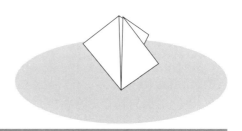

Long House 1 with eight **Foots**.

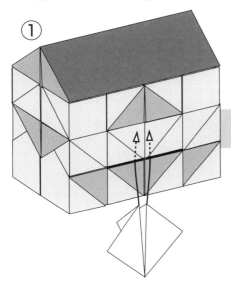

①

Insert between the space of the thick lines. It goes smoothly into the inside pockets of Basic Module A.

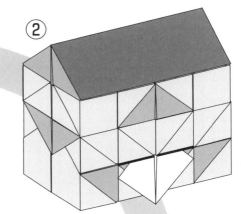

②

Completed

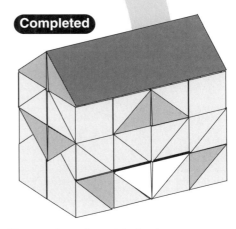

Fasten the other side in the same way.

Small House 2 with **Feet**

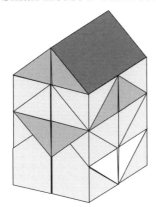

A small house fixed with the **fastener of foot**.

LARGE HOUSE

(Small House 2 with Foots$+A\times2+S\times2$
$+L_N+L_R+$**Additional Roofs)**

Extend **Small House 2**. I believe the
Additional Roof is a good idea. Once
you have mastered the method, try with
various sizes of basic houses and
additional roofs to make a variety of
houses.

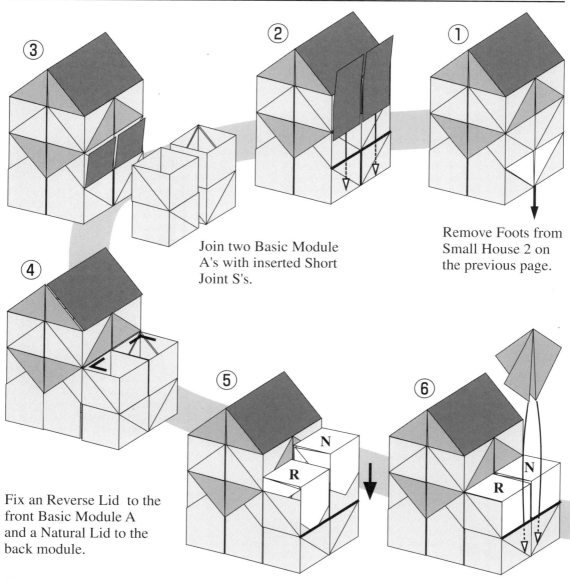

③

② Join two Basic Module
A's with inserted Short
Joint S's.

① Remove Foots from
Small House 2 on
the previous page.

④ Fix an Reverse Lid to the
front Basic Module A
and a Natural Lid to the
back module.

⑤

⑥

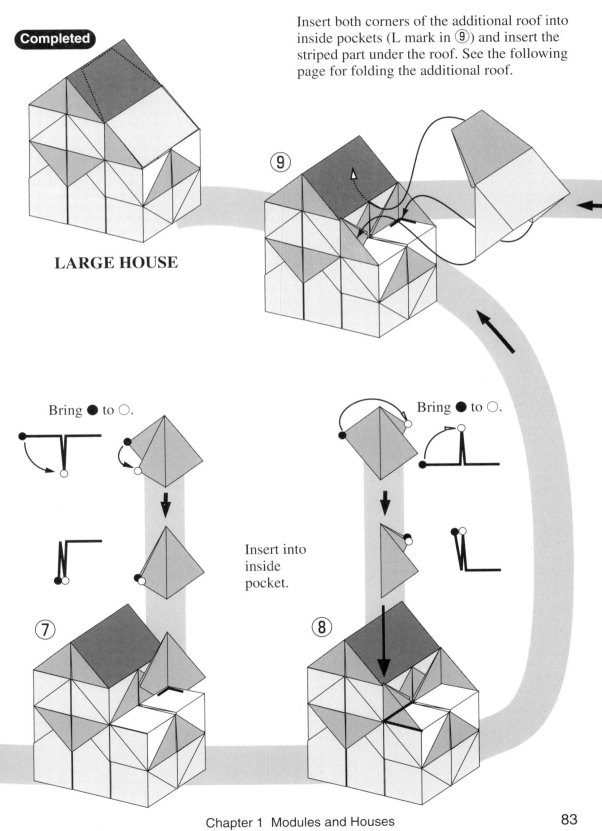

Completed

LARGE HOUSE

Insert both corners of the additional roof into inside pockets (L mark in ⑨) and insert the striped part under the roof. See the following page for folding the additional roof.

⑨

Bring ● to ○.

Insert into inside pocket.

⑦

Bring ● to ○.

⑧

ADDITIONAL ROOF

((6"/15 cm×5"/13 cm))

Open one side of Short Roof and refold.

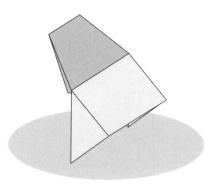

ADDITIONAL ROOF

To the previous page.

Short roof

Completed

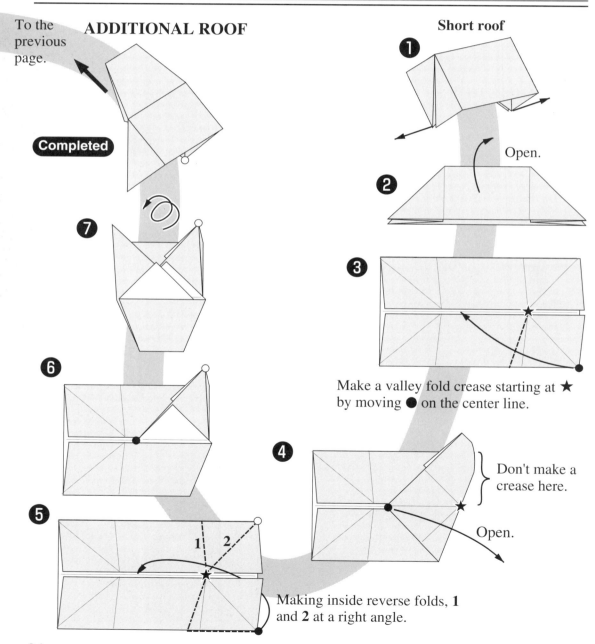

❶

Open.

❷

❸

Make a valley fold crease starting at ★ by moving ● on the center line.

❼

❻

❹

Don't make a crease here.

Open.

❺

1 **2**

Making inside reverse folds, **1** and **2** at a right angle.

1.9

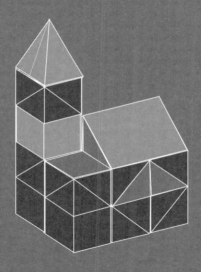

1.9 Small Church
Small Church

SMALL CHURCH

(Small House 2 + Steeple + A + LN + S×4)

Fix a spire to the pile construction of Basic Module A to make a steeple. Join the steeple to Small House 2 to make a Small Church.

SPIRE (P2)

First, make a spire of the steeple of a church.

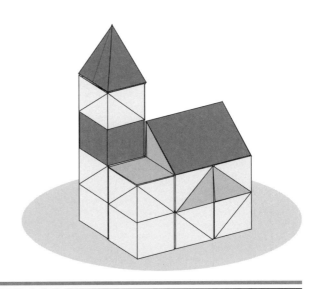

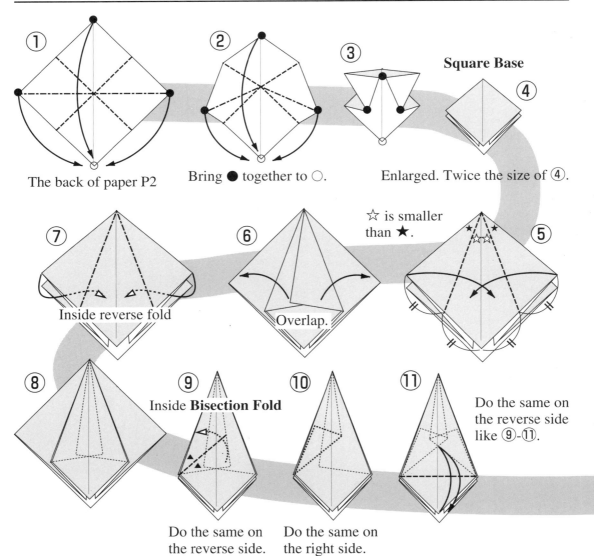

① The back of paper P2

② Bring ● together to ○.

③ **Square Base**

④ Enlarged. Twice the size of ④.

☆ is smaller than ★.

⑤

⑥ Overlap.

⑦ Inside reverse fold

⑧

⑨ Inside **Bisection Fold**
Do the same on the reverse side.

⑩ Do the same on the right side.

⑪ Do the same on the reverse side like ⑨-⑪.

STEEPLE

(A×2+T×2+Nail+Natural lid+ Spire)

To make a steeple, attach a natural lid and a nail to the pile construction of Basic Modules A and insert the three triangles of the spire between the space of the lid and module firmly. If you increase the number of the pile construct, you can make the steeple taller as much as you desire.

Fold in one of the tips ○ of the triangle.

Make a space between the lid and module and insert the three tips of the triangles in between.

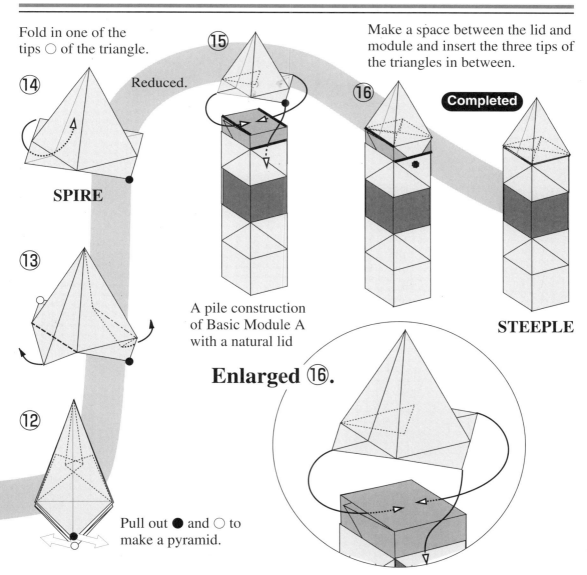

⑭

Reduced.

SPIRE

⑮

A pile construction of Basic Module A with a natural lid

⑯

Completed

STEEPLE

⑬

⑫

Pull out ● and ○ to make a pyramid.

Enlarged ⑯.

REINFORCEMENT OF THR SPIRE

The spire fixed according to the method on the previous page is not firm enough. To make it firm, use the following reinforcing component.

REINFORING COMPONENT OF THE SPIRE (P2×2)

Begin by opening Pile Joint T on page 24. Make two components. One is inserted into inside and the other into outside and insert the tip ● of the triangle under each other.

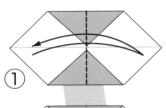

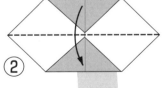

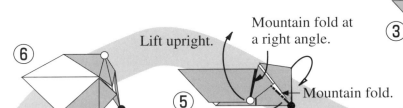

③ Fold the upper layer so that ★ meets ★.

④

⑤ Mountain fold at a right angle.

Lift upright.

Mountain fold.

⑥

REINFORCING COMPONENT OF A SPIRE

⑦ Let stand.

⑧ Insert into the slit of thick lines.

⑨

⑩ Insert into the outside pocket.

⑪

⑫

⑬

⑭ Fold the triangles of the spire and insert into each slit.

Completed

Insert the tip ● of the triangle under the component previously inserted.

CONSTRUCTION OF A SMALL CHURCH

To make a small church, join Small House 2, Steeple, Basic Module A with a Natural Lid with Short Joint S's.

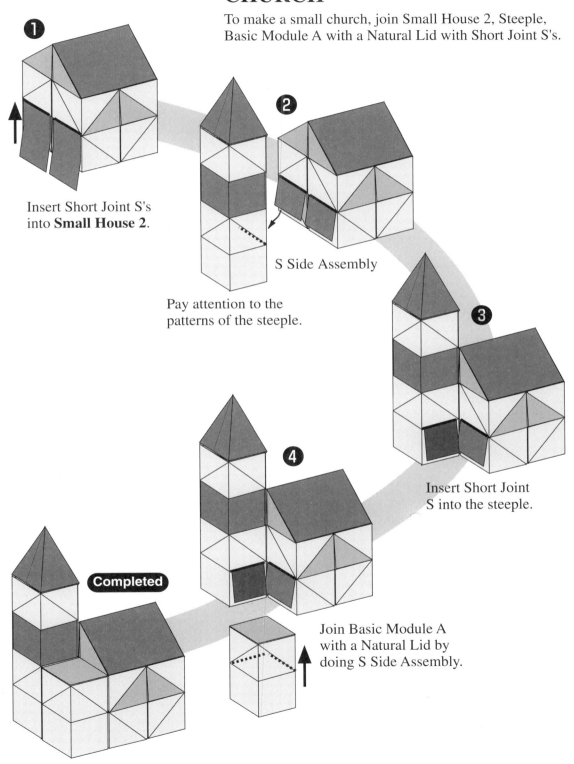

1 Insert Short Joint S's into **Small House 2**.

2 Pay attention to the patterns of the steeple.

S Side Assembly

3 Insert Short Joint S into the steeple.

4 Join Basic Module A with a Natural Lid by doing S Side Assembly.

Completed

SMALL CHURCH

MASS PRODUCTION 4 (TIPS FOR CUTTING)

There is an efficient methods to cut the creased paper of Mass Productions 1-3 into 16.

From **Mass Productions 1 - 3** on pages 36, 65 and 66.

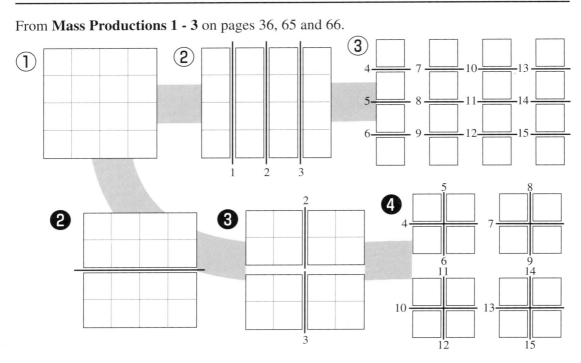

In the above methods, you have to cut 15 times, which are inefficient. You could place paper one upon another and cut together to save your trouble. But the paper easily moves, and you are unable to obtain satisfactory results. Then try the following method.

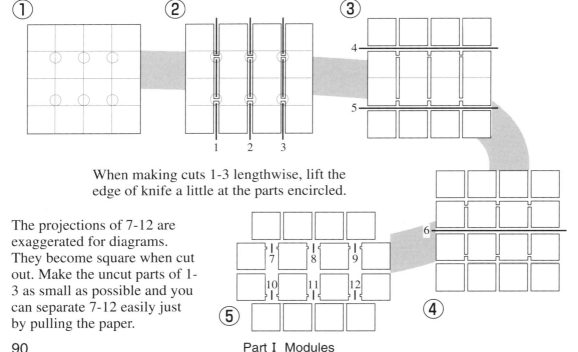

When making cuts 1-3 lengthwise, lift the edge of knife a little at the parts encircled.

The projections of 7-12 are exaggerated for diagrams. They become square when cut out. Make the uncut parts of 1-3 as small as possible and you can separate 7-12 easily just by pulling the paper.

1.10

1.10 Greek Shrine
**The Pillar of a Greek Shrine
Octagonal Module
The Floor of a Greek Shrine**

THE PILLAR OF A GREEK SHRINE

(A×3＋U×4＋Lid＋Slate＋Component for fixing slate×2)

The pillar of a Greek shrine is made up of stones, which were quarried in the shape of cylinder and piled up. Each horizontal section of the stones has a hole in the middle. A strong wooden bar is inserted into the hole to prevent the pillar from collapsing. The pillar in the right consists of three piles of octagonal Basic Module A's with a slate (square board) on top. The middle hole in the section of lying pillar is the hole to prevent from tilting, as mentioned above.

OCTAGONAL MODULE (A)

This is a Basic Module A with four creases added vertically.

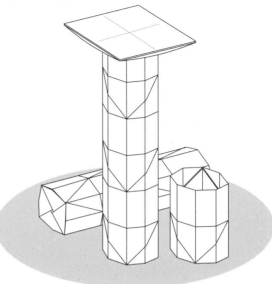

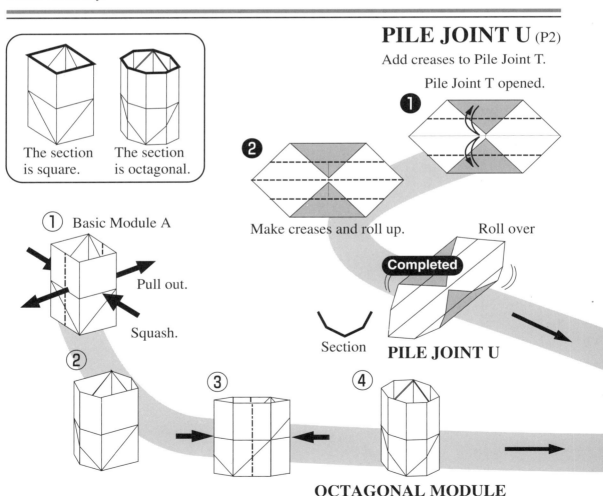

The section is square.

The section is octagonal.

① Basic Module A

Pull out.

Squash.

② ③ ④

OCTAGONAL MODULE

PILE JOINT U (P2)

Add creases to Pile Joint T.

Pile Joint T opened.

①

② Make creases and roll up.

Roll over

Completed

Section

PILE JOINT U

HOW TO PUT A LID ON THE OCTAGONAL MODULE

Return the octagonal pillar to a square pillar and put a lid on.

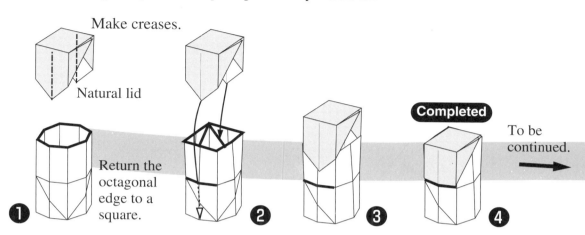

Make creases.

Natural lid

1 Return the octagonal edge to a square.

2

3

Completed

4

To be continued.

PILE CONSTRUCTION OF OCTAGONAL MODULES

The same as Basic Module A's.

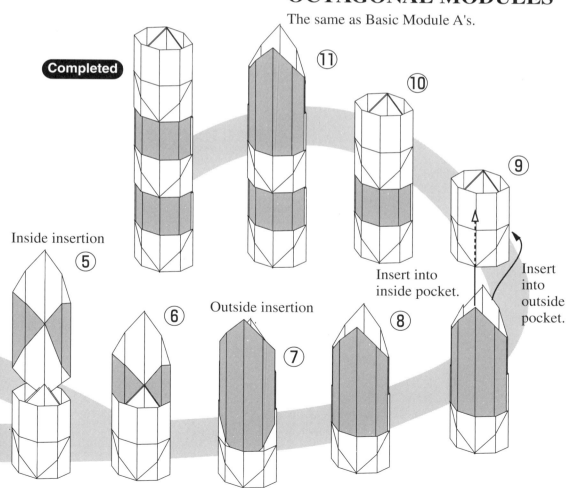

Completed

11

10

9

Insert into inside pocket.

Insert into outside pocket.

Inside insertion

5

6

Outside insertion

7

8

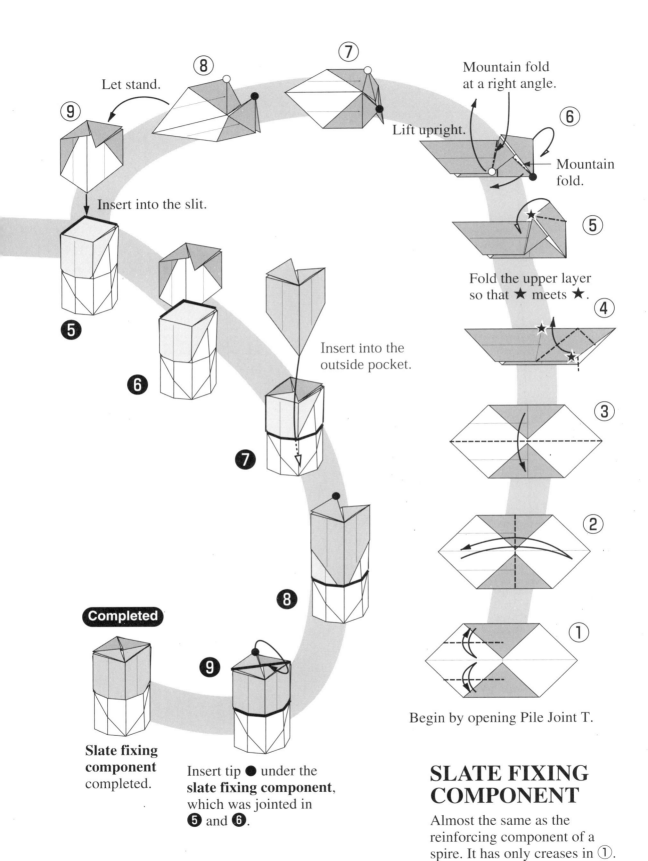

Let stand.

Insert into the slit.

5

6

Insert into the
outside pocket.

7

8

9

Insert tip ● under the
slate fixing component,
which was jointed in
5 and **6**.

Mountain fold
at a right angle.

6

Lift upright.

Mountain
fold.

5

Fold the upper layer
so that ★ meets ★.

4

3

2

1

Begin by opening Pile Joint T.

SLATE FIXING
COMPONENT

Almost the same as the
reinforcing component of a
spire. It has only creases in ①.

Completed

**Slate fixing
component** completed.

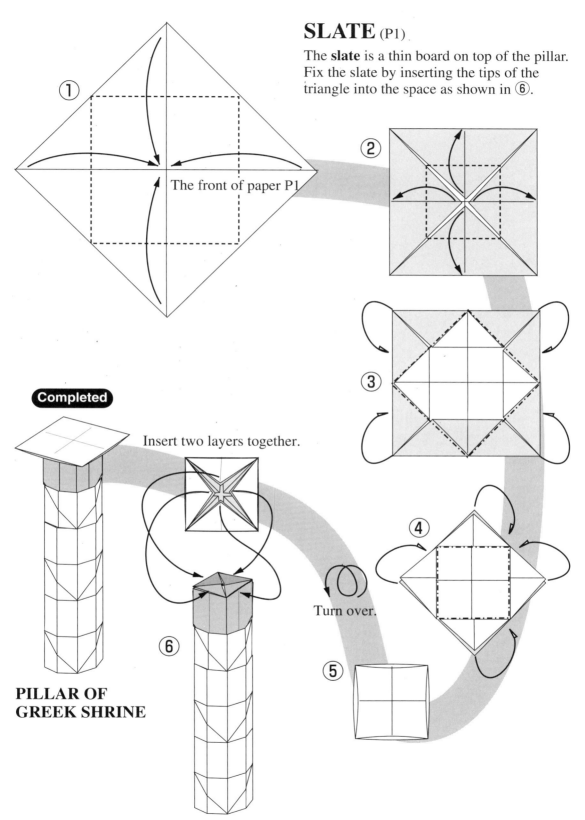

SLATE (P1)

The **slate** is a thin board on top of the pillar. Fix the slate by inserting the tips of the triangle into the space as shown in ⑥.

The front of paper P1

Completed

Insert two layers together.

Turn over.

PILLAR OF GREEK SHRINE

The **pillar** with a **lid** and a **slate fixing component**

THE FLOOR OF THE GREEK SHRINE

Make the floor by **S Side Assembly** of Basic Module A's with lids. It is also possible to make it by **J Side Assembly**. The **pillar of the Greek shrine** is set up on the floor with Pile Joint T.

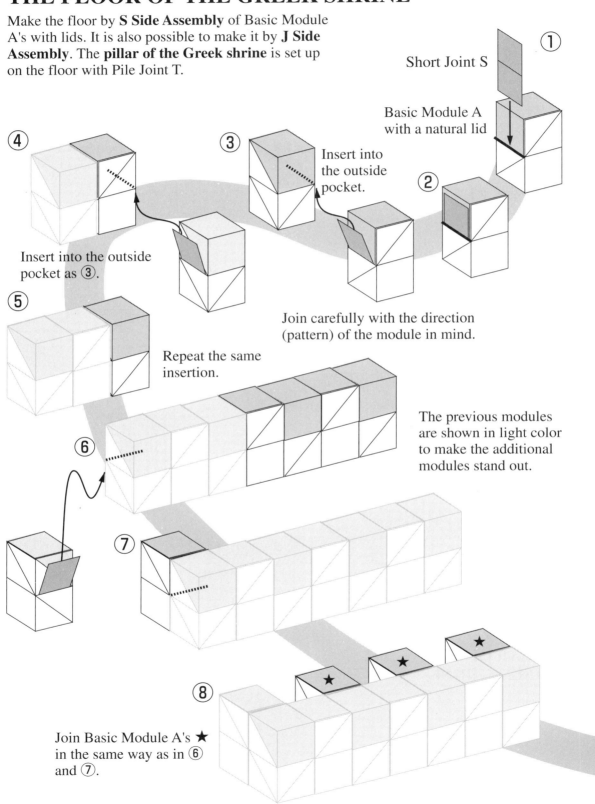

Short Joint S

①

Basic Module A with a natural lid

②

③ Insert into the outside pocket.

④ Insert into the outside pocket as ③.

Join carefully with the direction (pattern) of the module in mind.

⑤ Repeat the same insertion.

The previous modules are shown in light color to make the additional modules stand out.

⑥

⑦

⑧ Join Basic Module A's ★ in the same way as in ⑥ and ⑦.

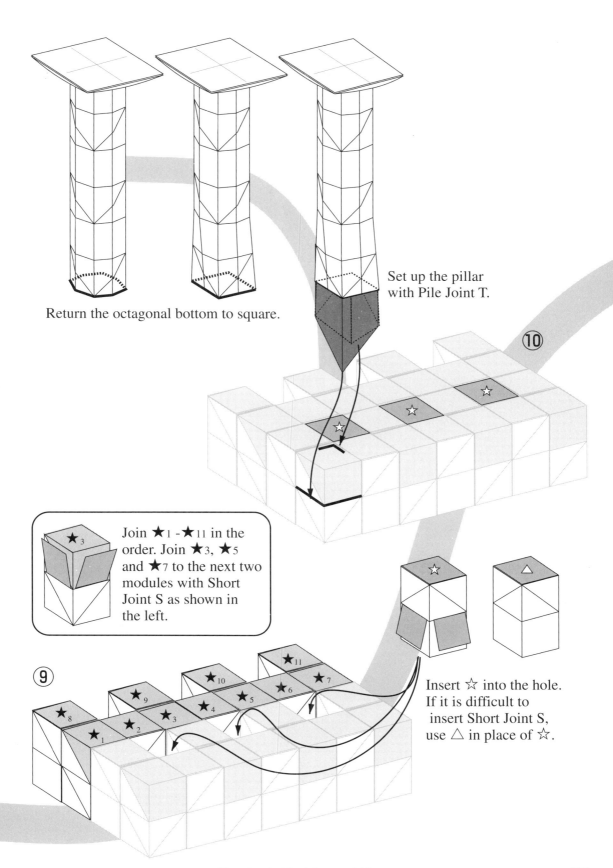

Return the octagonal bottom to square.

Set up the pillar with Pile Joint T.

⑩

Join ★1 -★11 in the order. Join ★3, ★5 and ★7 to the next two modules with Short Joint S as shown in the left.

Insert ☆ into the hole. If it is difficult to insert Short Joint S, use △ in place of ☆.

⑨

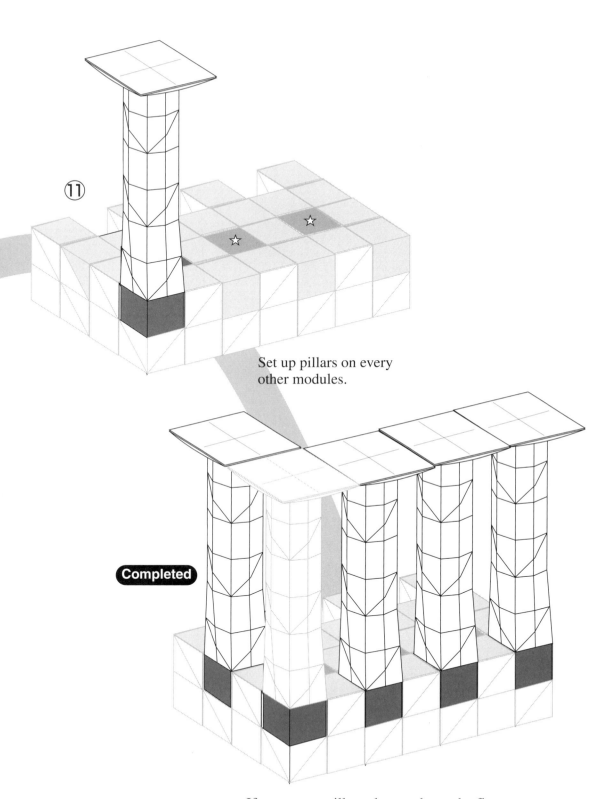

⑪

Set up pillars on every
other modules.

Completed

If you set up pillars alternately on the floor
of square modules, you can make a Greek
shrine. You may change the interval
between pillars and their height as desired.

2.1

Chapter 2 Geometrical Form

2.1 Twist Construction
Twist Construction
Twist Joint
Natural and Reverse Twist Modules
Mixed Construction of Natural and Reverse Twist Modules

TWIST CONSTRUCTION

Basic Module A's jointed by a twist joint.

TWIST JOINT (P2)

The joint is used for **Twist Construction**. There are two kinds of joints, **Natural Twist Joint N** and **Reverse Twist Joint R**.

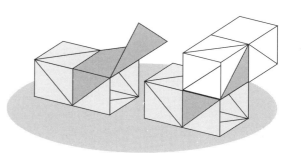

The back of paper P2

①

② ❷

③ ❸

Open at a right angle.

④ ❹

Completed

NATURAL TWIST JOINT N

REVERSE TWIST JOINT R

TWIST CONSTRUCTION

Just insert the joint into **outside pockets**.

⑤

Natural Twist Joint N

⑥ ⑦ ⑧ ⑨

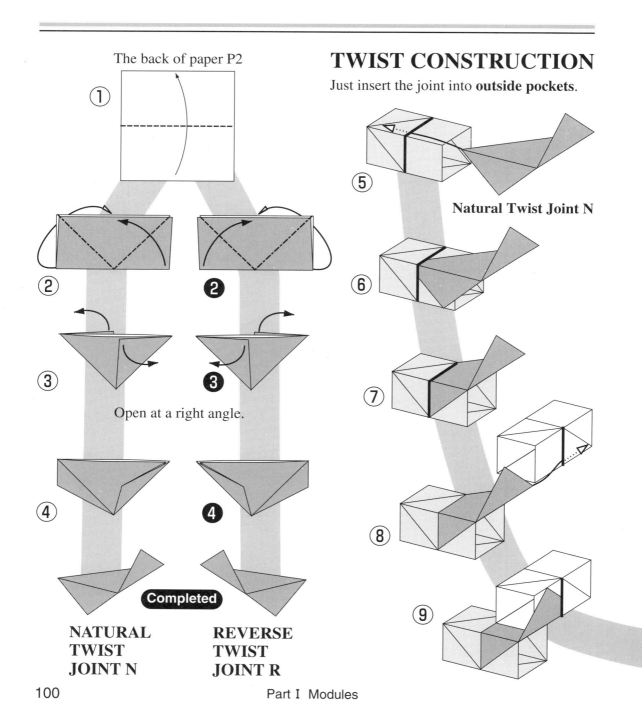

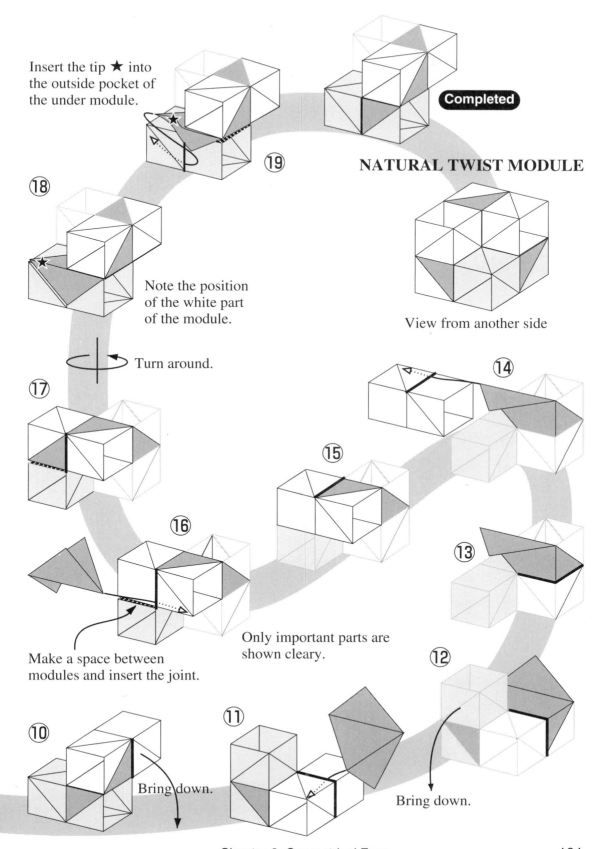

Insert the tip ★ into
the outside pocket of
the under module.

⑲

Completed

⑱

NATURAL TWIST MODULE

Note the position
of the white part
of the module.

View from another side

Turn around.

⑰

⑭

⑮

⑯

⑬

Only important parts are
shown cleary.

⑫

Make a space between
modules and insert the joint.

⑩

⑪

Bring down.

Bring down.

NATURAL AND REVERSE TWIST MODULES

If you use **Reverse Twist Joint R** in place of **Natural Twist Joint N**, you can make **Reverse Twist Module**, which is the mirror image of **Natural Twist Module**.

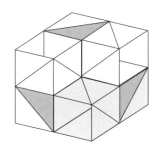

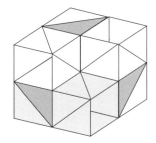

NATURAL TWIST MODULE   REVERSE TWIST MODULE

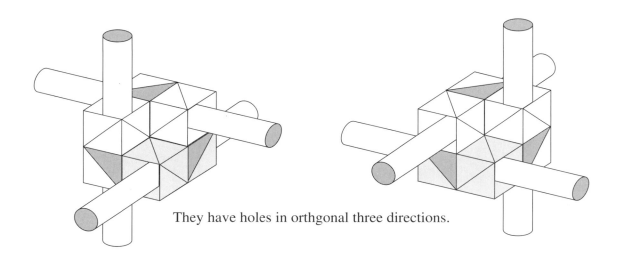

They have holes in orthgonal three directions.

Problem 2.1-1

(1) Join additional Basic Module A's to both ends of each Natural Twist Module with Pile Joint T's.

(2) Join two Natural Twist Modules with Pile Joint T.

(3) Join four Natural Twist Modules with Pile Joint T's.

(4) Join eight Natural Twist Modules with Pile Joint T's.

Answer to (1)

Bring an additional module to the above position as if passing a bar through the hole and join. **Pile Joint T** is shown in dark color.

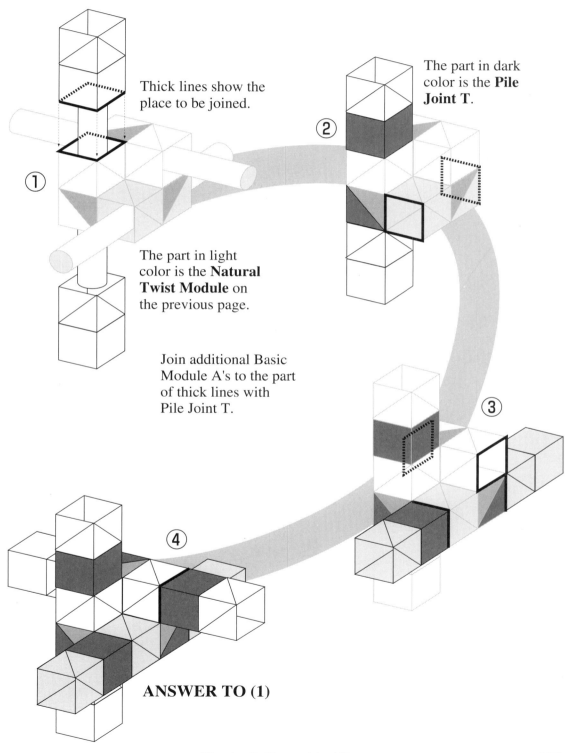

Thick lines show the place to be joined.

The part in light color is the **Natural Twist Module** on the previous page.

The part in dark color is the **Pile Joint T**.

Join additional Basic Module A's to the part of thick lines with Pile Joint T.

ANSWER TO (1)

Answer to (2), (3) and (4)

Couple the thick lines and join with Pile Joint T. ❸ and ❺ are difficult, so join with particular care.

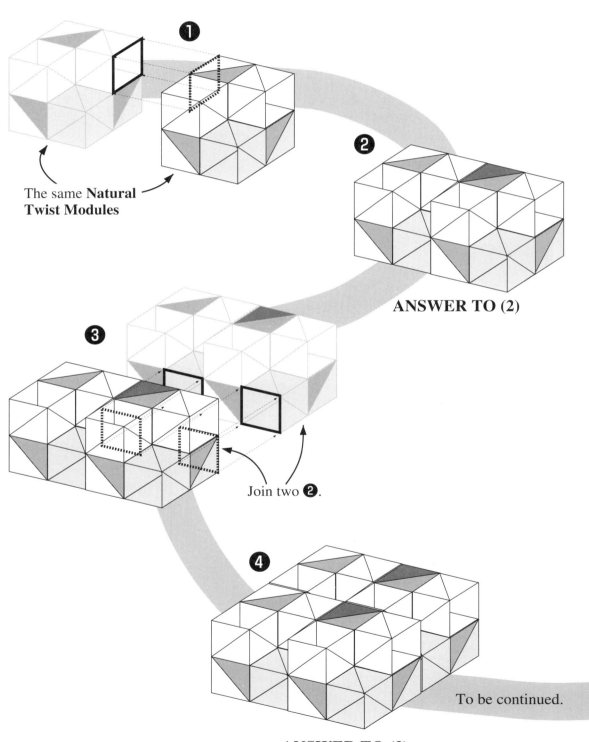

The same **Natural Twist Modules**

ANSWER TO (2)

Join two ❷.

To be continued.

ANSWER TO (3)

Part I Modules

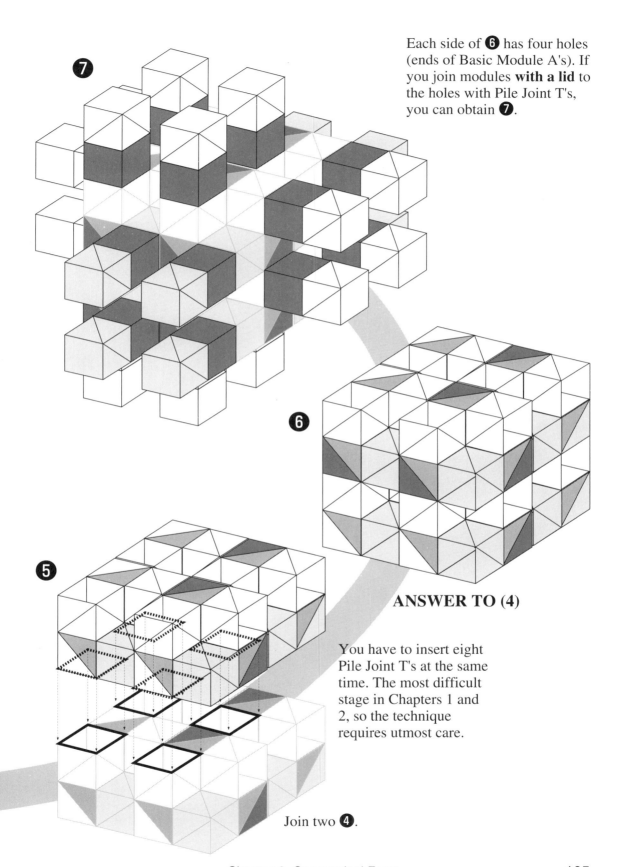

⑦

Each side of **⑥** has four holes (ends of Basic Module A's). If you join modules **with a lid** to the holes with Pile Joint T's, you can obtain **⑦**.

⑥

ANSWER TO (4)

⑤

You have to insert eight Pile Joint T's at the same time. The most difficult stage in Chapters 1 and 2, so the technique requires utmost care.

Join two **④**.

Chapter 2 Geometrical Form   105

MIXED CONSTRUCTION OF NATURAL AND REVERSE TWIST MODULES

Assemble **Natural Twist Module** and **Reverse Twist Module**. You can join them with Pile Joint T as you have done so far. There are a variety of joining methods, but introduced here is the most orthodox one.

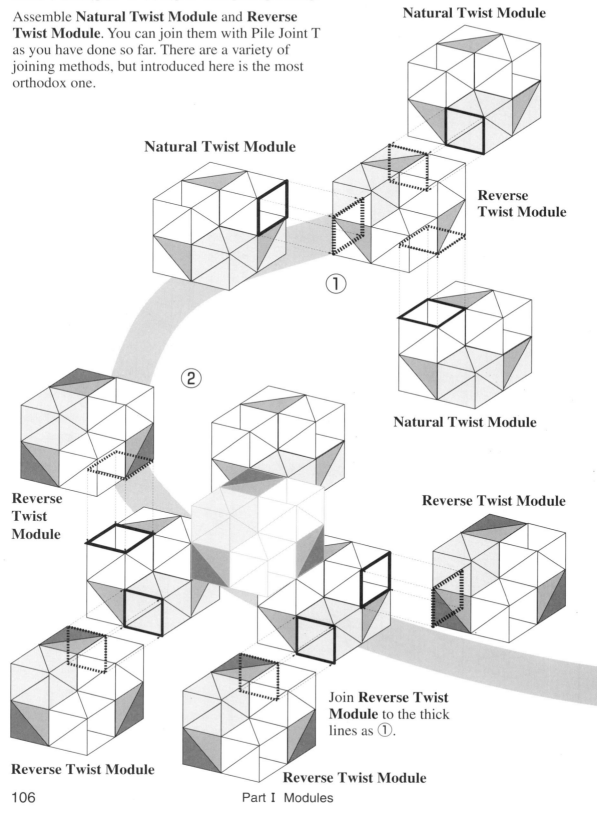

Natural Twist Module

Natural Twist Module

Reverse Twist Module

Natural Twist Module

Reverse Twist Module

Reverse Twist Module

Reverse Twist Module

Join **Reverse Twist Module** to the thick lines as ①.

Reverse Twist Module

Reverse Twist Module

Part I Modules

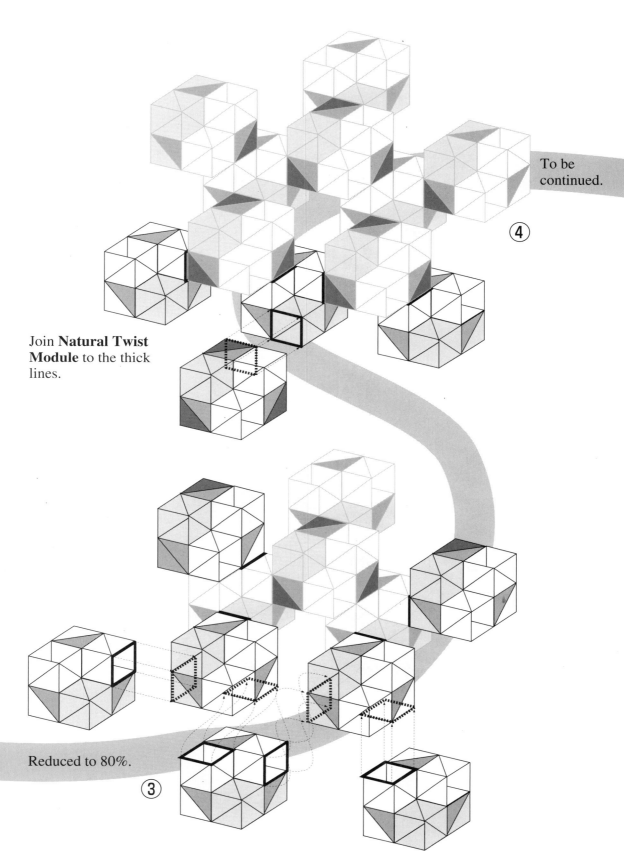

To be
continued.

④

Join **Natural Twist Module** to the thick lines.

③

Reduced to 80%.

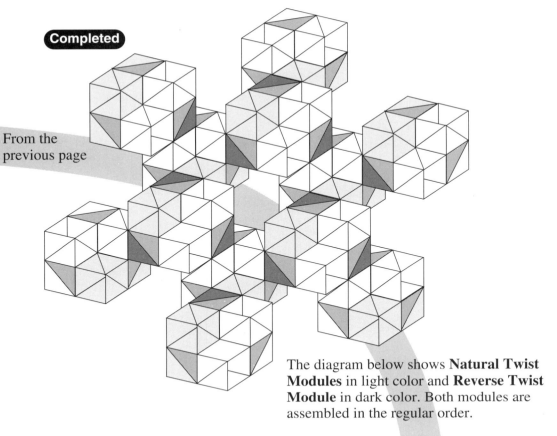

From the
previous page

The diagram below shows **Natural Twist
Modules** in light color and **Reverse Twist
Module** in dark color. Both modules are
assembled in the regular order.

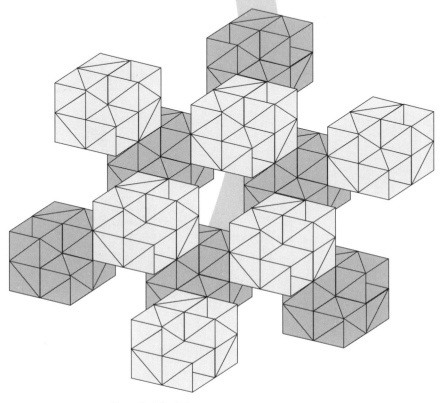

　　　　Part I　Modules

2.2

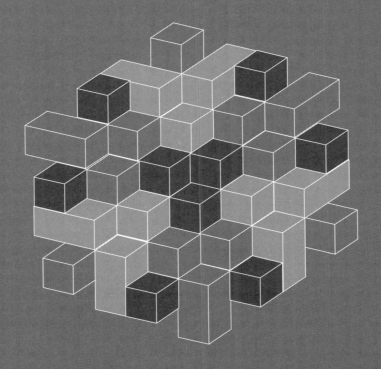

2.2 Hexagonal Construction
Hexagonal Construction
Snow Flakes

P.25

HEXAGONAL CONSTRUCTION

If you join Simple Module B with a lid with **Hook Joint F** in order, you can automatically complete **Hexagonal Construction**. The **Hexagonal Module** on the right consists of three modules. You may also use Basic Module A with a nail in place of Simple Module B.

HOOK JOINT F

Fold **Long Joint L** in half at a right angle.

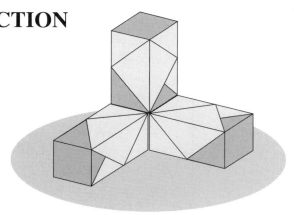

Fold **Long Joint L** (p. 24)

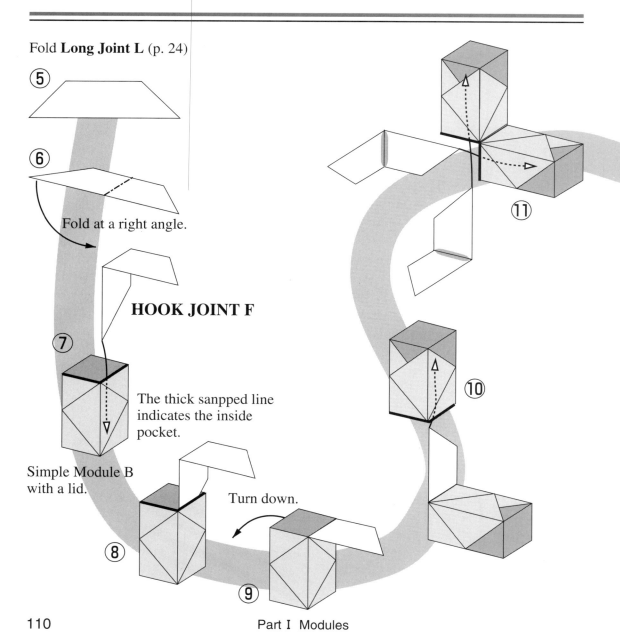

⑤

⑥

Fold at a right angle.

HOOK JOINT F

⑦

The thick sanpped line indicates the inside pocket.

Simple Module B with a lid.

⑧

Turn down.

⑨

⑩

⑪

Part I Modules

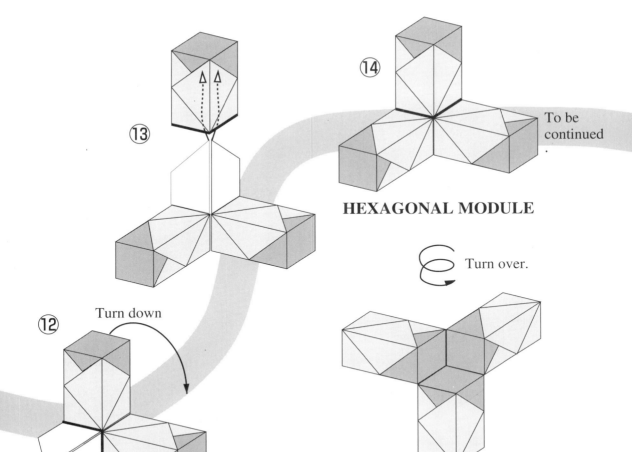

⑬

⑫ Turn down

⑭

To be continued

HEXAGONAL MODULE

Turn over.

The back of ⑭

SNOW FLAKES

Make two **Hexagonal Modules** with white paper and pile them up. Use smaller paper, if possible.

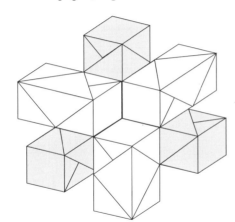

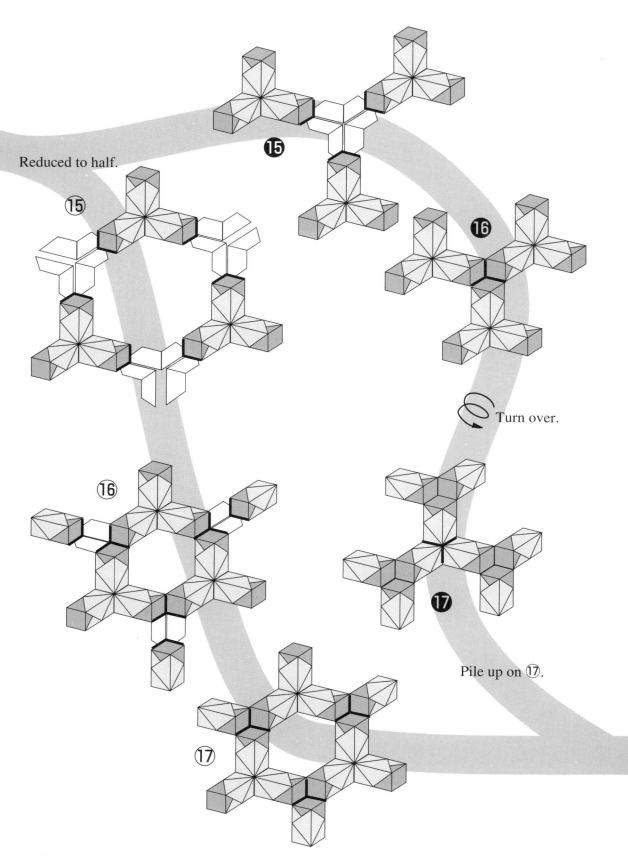

Reduced to half.

⑮

⑮

⑯

Turn over.

⑯

⑰

Pile up on ⑰.

⑰

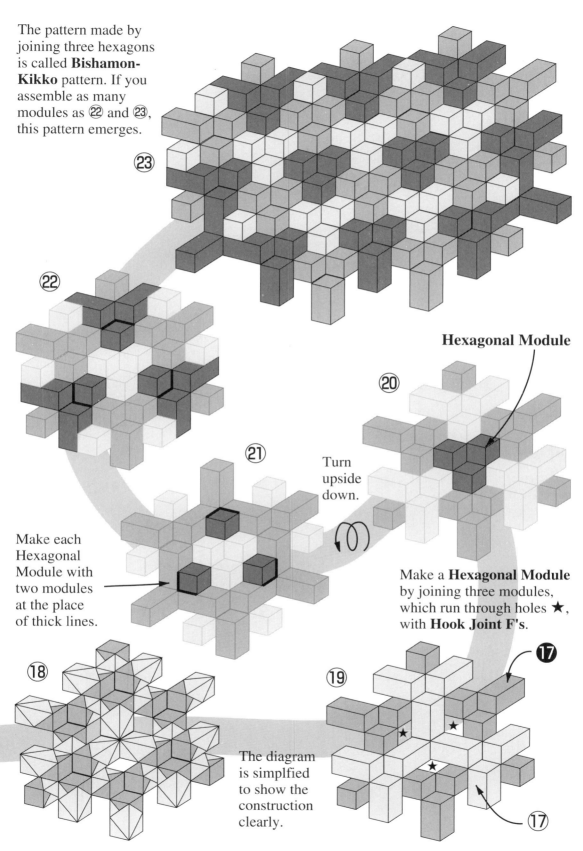

The pattern made by joining three hexagons is called **Bishamon-Kikko** pattern. If you assemble as many modules as ㉒ and ㉓, this pattern emerges.

㉓

㉒

Hexagonal Module

㉒

Turn upside down.

Make each Hexagonal Module with two modules at the place of thick lines.

Make a **Hexagonal Module** by joining three modules, which run through holes ★, with **Hook Joint F's**.

⓲

⓳

⓱

The diagram is simplfied to show the construction clearly.

⑰

COFFEE BREAK

You must be tired. Now let's have a rest before going to Part 2. A cup of coffee will take away your tiredness.

COFFEE BEAN

(Japanese paper: 1/2"/1.5 cm×3/4"/2 cm)

This is an application of the technique for folding a boat. Use small brown Japanese paper. The size is about 1/2"/1.5 cm×3/4"/2 cm. The positions and angles of folding lines are rather free.

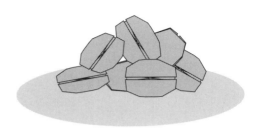

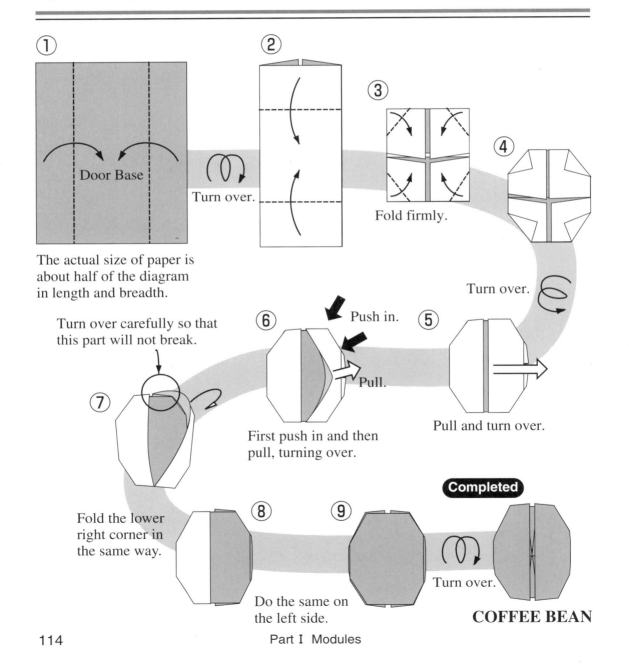

① Door Base

The actual size of paper is about half of the diagram in length and breadth.

Turn over.

②

③ Fold firmly.

④

Turn over.

⑤ Pull and turn over.

Push in.

Pull.

⑥ First push in and then pull, turning over.

Turn over carefully so that this part will not break.

⑦

Fold the lower right corner in the same way.

⑧ Do the same on the left side.

⑨ Turn over.

Completed

COFFEE BEAN

Part II Rose

Twist Fold
Rose Bud
Rose
Four Leaves
Rose Leaves
Pyramid

TWIST FOLD

Twist and squash the middle where pleats meet. This is a Twist Fold in the right diagram. Make creases crosswise in advance as ①. Mitsuhiro Uchiyama developed this method into beautiful **Kamon-ori** (flower crest). Yoshihide Momotani and Shuzo Fujimoto created **Hira-ori (crystallographic origami)** by joining Twist Folds (Reference:[U],[Mo],[F]). The **Rose Bud** on page 118 is a 3D model of Twist Fold.

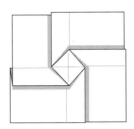

THE MECHANISM OF A TWIST FOLD

The pleats meet in the middle loosely. Twist and squash this middle neatly. Pleats can be made more than three, but it is simple and easy to fold four pleats which cross at right angles.

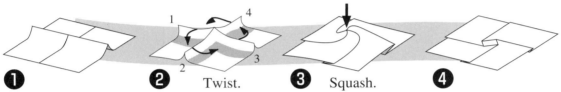

❶   ❷ Twist.   ❸ Squash.   ❹

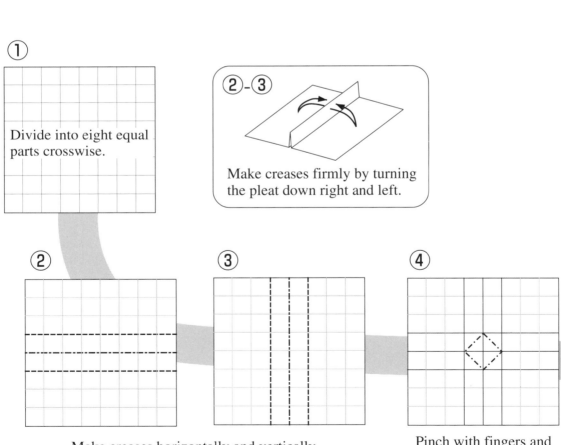

① Divide into eight equal parts crosswise.

②-③ Make creases firmly by turning the pleat down right and left.

② ③ Make creases horizontally and vertically.

④ Pinch with fingers and make mountain folds.

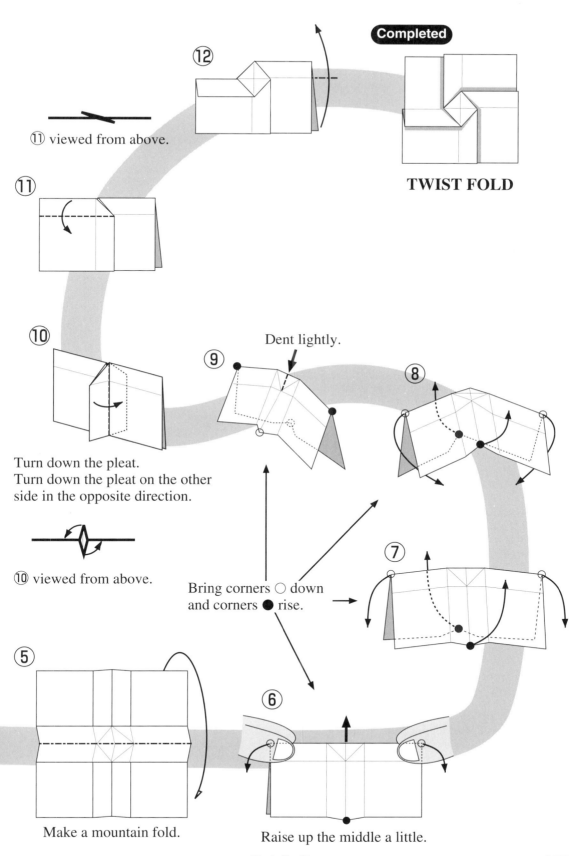

Completed

⑫

⑪ viewed from above.

⑪

TWIST FOLD

⑩

⑨ Dent lightly.

⑧

Turn down the pleat.
Turn down the pleat on the other
side in the opposite direction.

⑩ viewed from above.

Bring corners ○ down
and corners ● rise.

⑦

⑤

⑥

Make a mountain fold.

Raise up the middle a little.

Part Ⅱ Rose   117

ROSE BUD (P1)

If you make **Twist Fold** three-dimensional and gather the corners of paper, you can obtain **Rose Bud**. To fold the sepals neatly, divide the paper into eight equal parts.

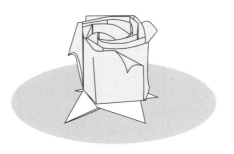

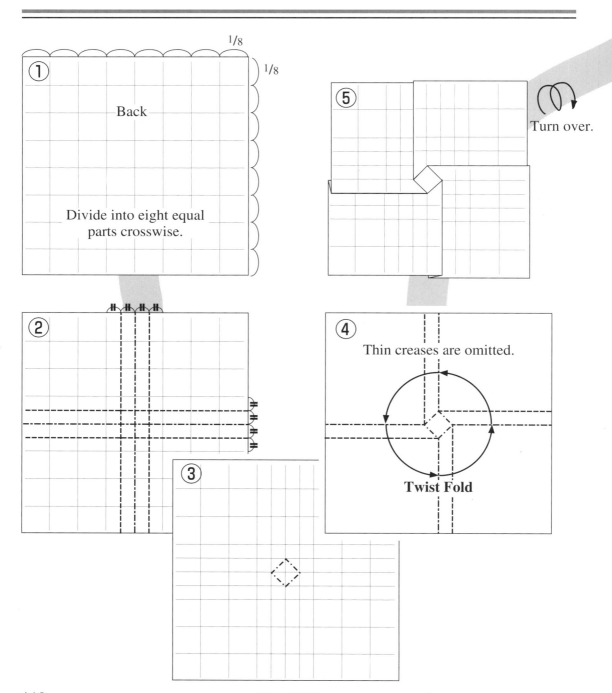

① Back

Divide into eight equal parts crosswise.

1/8

1/8

②

③

④ Thin creases are omitted.

Twist Fold

⑤ Turn over.

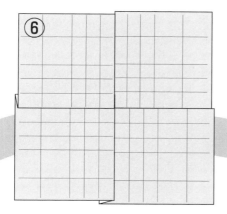

⑥

Align the right edge with the thick line.

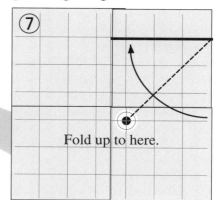

⑦

Fold up to here.

Make the other three creases
in the same way.

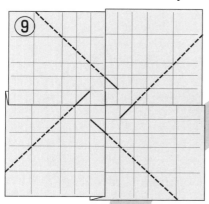

⑨

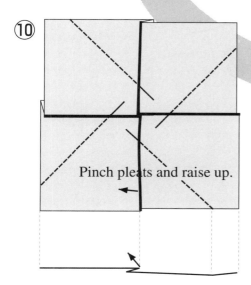

⑧

Make a crease
here.

Warning!
Never fold here.

In the following diagrams,
thin creases are omitted.

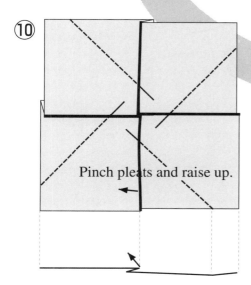

⑩

Pinch pleats and raise up.

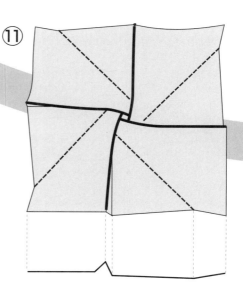

⑪

The pleat viewed from the side

The pleat viewed from the side

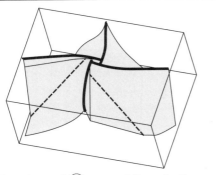

The view of ⑬ seen obliquely from above. The thick curved lines are on the surface of the rectangle of the rectangular parallelepiped.

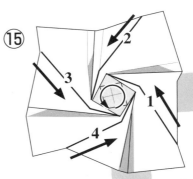

Pinch the four pleats and push in the direction of arrows little by little so that the center rotates.

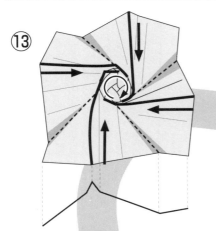

The pleat viewed from the side

Pinch the pleats and push lightly from both sides so that the center revolves in the direction of arrows.

Turn over.

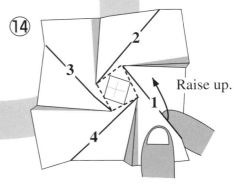

Raise up.

Pinch **mountain-fold creases 1-4** and raise up little by little. Make sure that the square **valley-fold creases** in the center are made neatly.

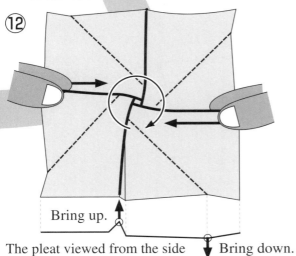

Bring up.

The pleat viewed from the side   Bring down.

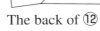

The back of ⑫

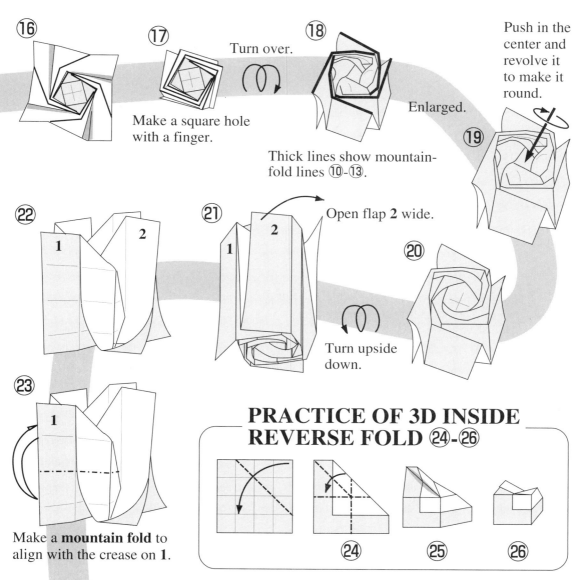

⑯ Make a square hole with a finger.

⑰ Turn over.

⑱ Thick lines show mountain-fold lines ⑩-⑬.

Enlarged.

Push in the center and revolve it to make it round.

⑲

⑳

㉑ Open flap **2** wide.

Turn upside down.

㉒

㉓ Make a **mountain fold** to align with the crease on **1**.

PRACTICE OF 3D INSIDE REVERSE FOLD ㉔-㉖

㉔ ㉕ ㉖

If you find it difficult to fold like this, practice as shown above.

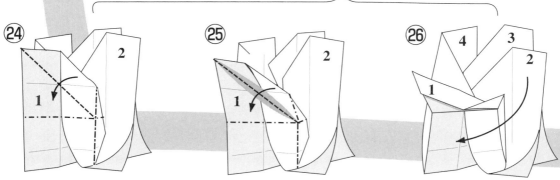

㉔

㉕

3D INSIDE REVERSE FOLD

㉖ Turn round at an angle of 90 degrees and fold **2** in the same way.

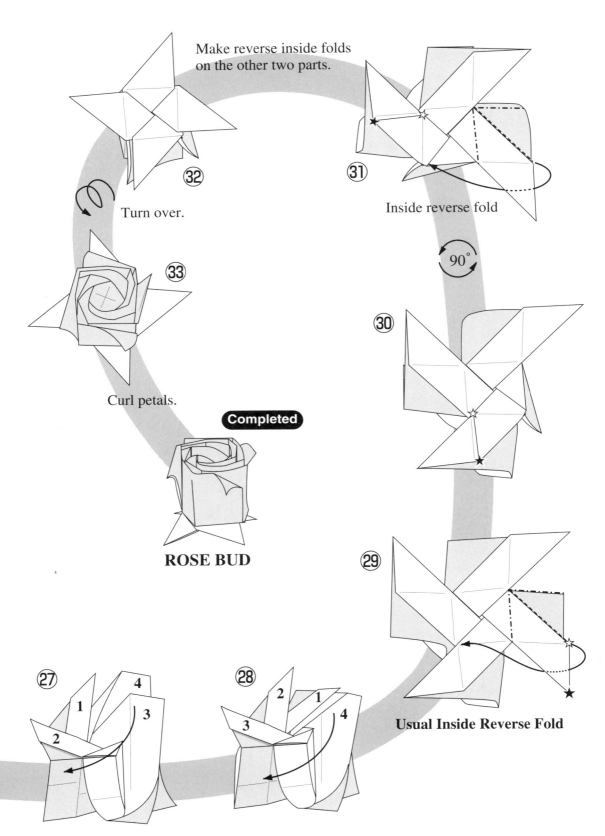

Make reverse inside folds
on the other two parts.

㉜

Turn over.

Inside reverse fold

㉛

90°

㉝

㉚

Curl petals.

Completed

㉙

ROSE BUD

Usual Inside Reverse Fold

㉗ 1 4 3 2

㉘ 2 1 4 3

Fold **3** and **4** in the same way.

Part Ⅱ Rose

ROSE

(Japanese paper: about 8"/20 cm × 8"/20 cm)

The basic structure is the same as **Rose Bud**, but oblique creases and the processes of increasing petals ⑰-⑲ are very difficult.

Challenge this Rose only after you have mastered Rose Bud. If you succeed in folding this Rose, you are sure to win admiration from other origami lovers. Don't let failures discourage you! The point is to read the explanations carefully without skipping them.

① Front

② Align the edges of paper with the center line.

③ Move a little.

④

⑤ Enlarged twice.

⑥ Fold together in half.

⑦

⑧ Open.

⑨ Fold the lower half in the same way as steps ④-⑧.

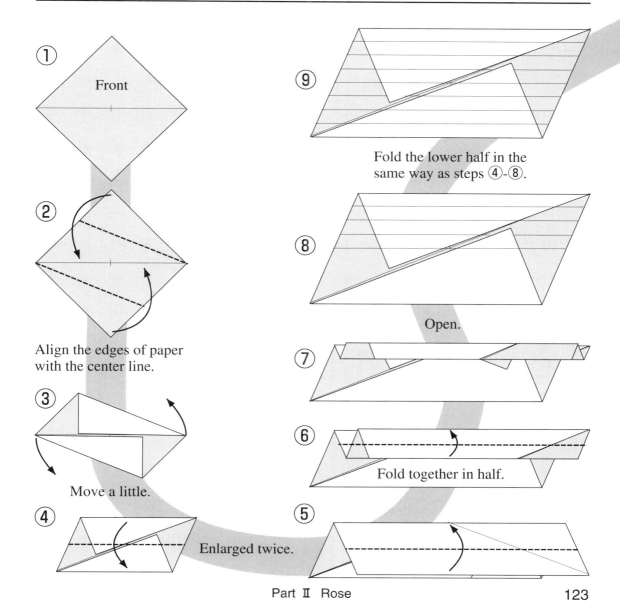

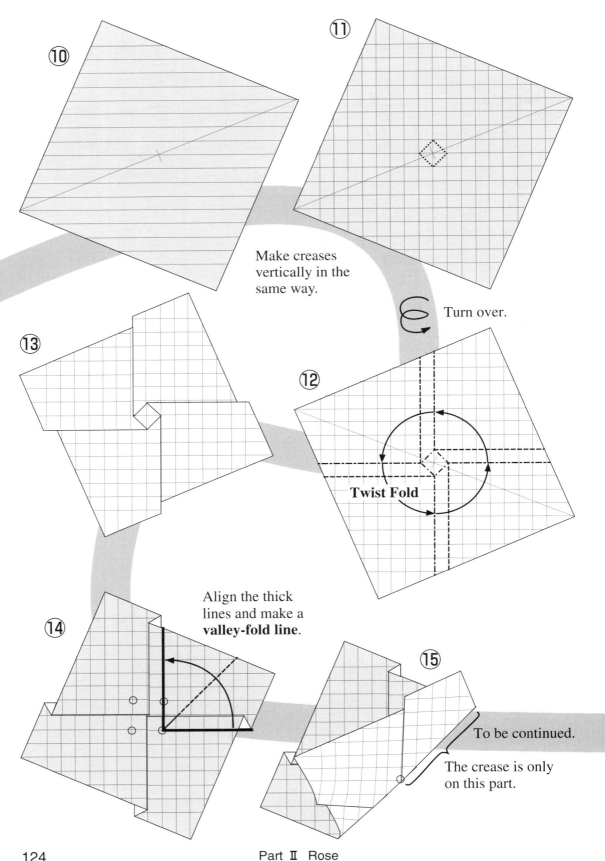

⑩

⑪

Make creases
vertically in the
same way.

Turn over.

⑬

⑫

Twist Fold

⑭

Align the thick
lines and make a
valley-fold line.

⑮

To be continued.

The crease is only
on this part.

Part Ⅱ Rose

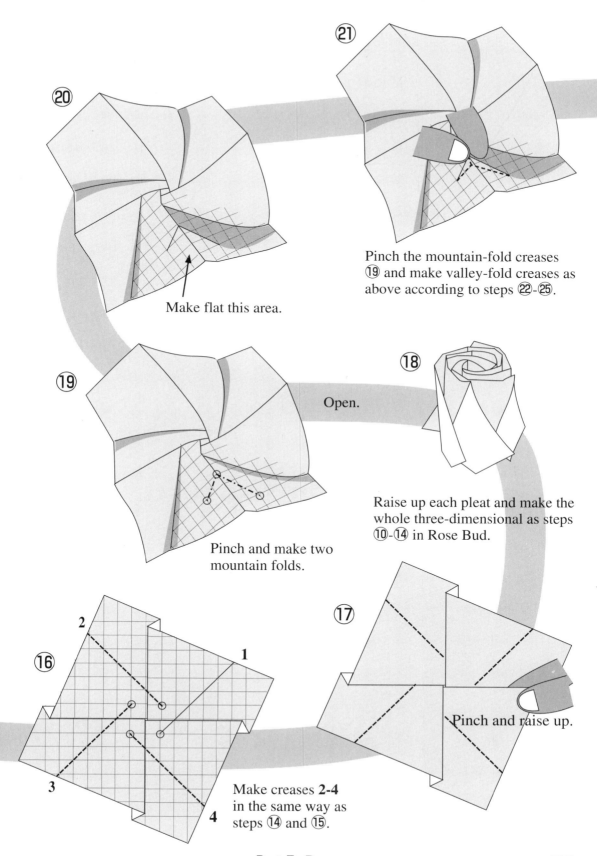

㉑ Pinch the mountain-fold creases ⑲ and make valley-fold creases as above according to steps ㉒-㉕.

⑳ Make flat this area.

Open.

⑲ Pinch and make two mountain folds.

⑱ Raise up each pleat and make the whole three-dimensional as steps ⑩-⑭ in Rose Bud.

⑯ Make creases **2-4** in the same way as steps ⑭ and ⑮.

⑰ Pinch and raise up.

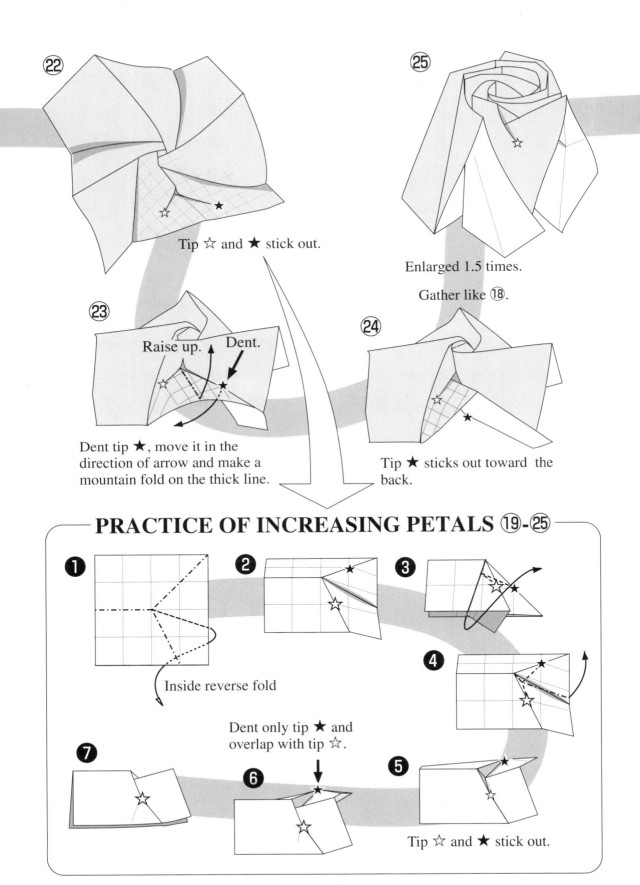

㉒ Tip ☆ and ★ stick out.

㉓ Raise up. Dent.

Dent tip ★, move it in the direction of arrow and make a mountain fold on the thick line.

㉔ Tip ★ sticks out toward the back.

㉕ Enlarged 1.5 times.

Gather like ⑱.

PRACTICE OF INCREASING PETALS ⑲-㉕

❶ Inside reverse fold

❷

❸

❹

Dent only tip ★ and overlap with tip ☆.

❺ Tip ☆ and ★ stick out.

❻

❼

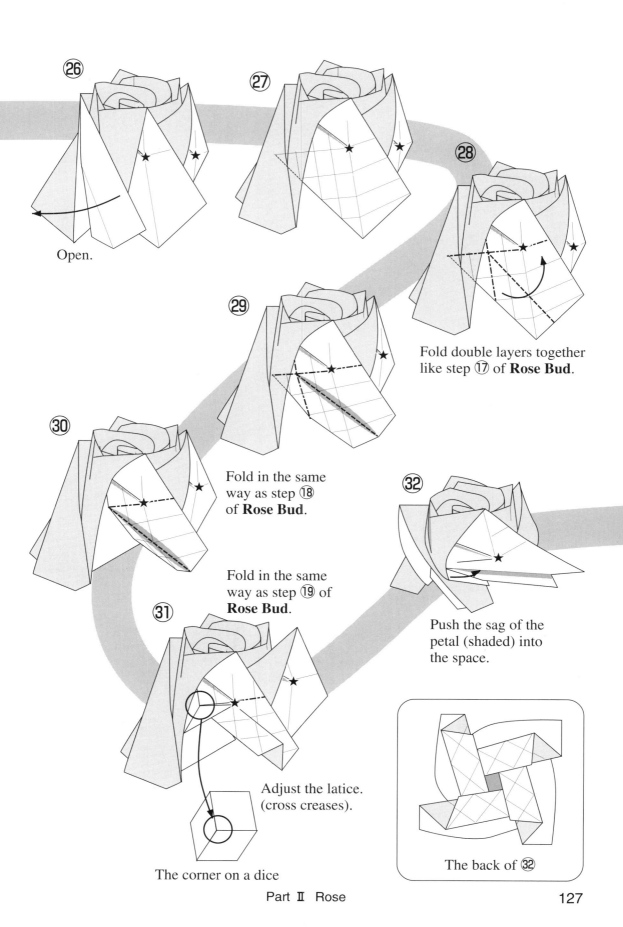

㉖

Open.

㉗

㉘

Fold double layers together like step ⑰ of **Rose Bud**.

㉙

㉚

Fold in the same way as step ⑱ of **Rose Bud**.

Fold in the same way as step ⑲ of **Rose Bud**.

㉛

Adjust the latice. (cross creases).

The corner on a dice

㉜

Push the sag of the petal (shaded) into the space.

The back of ㉜

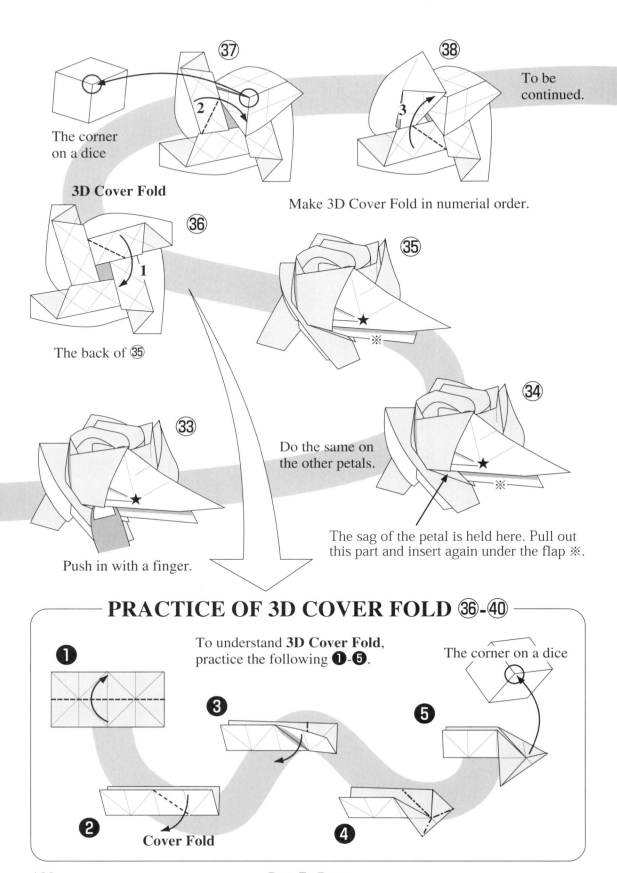

㊲

The corner
on a dice

2

3D Cover Fold

㊱

1

The back of ㉟

㊳

To be
continued.

Make 3D Cover Fold in numerial order.

3

㉟

★

※

㉞

Do the same on
the other petals.

★

※

㉝

★

Push in with a finger.

The sag of the petal is held here. Pull out
this part and insert again under the flap ※.

PRACTICE OF 3D COVER FOLD ㊱-㊵

❶

To understand **3D Cover Fold**,
practice the following ❶-❺.

The corner on a dice

❸

❺

❷

Cover Fold

❹

③⑨

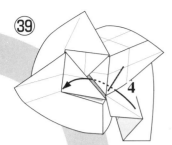

4

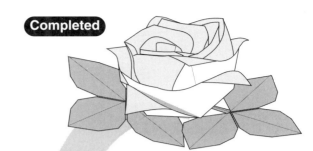

Insert the stem of **Rose Leaves** (p. 116) between the space of the flower bottom.

④⓪

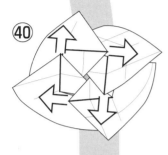

Bravo! You must be tired.

Pull out firmly in the direction of arrows, making **mountain folds** on the thick lines and make the flower bottom square.

Arrange the corner as step ⑲ of **Rose Bud**.

④⑤

④①

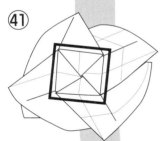

The flower bottom is square.

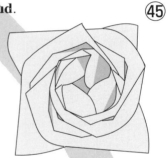

The view from above

Turn over.

④②

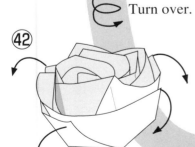

④④

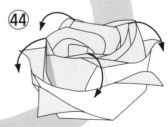

Curl the inside petals.

④③

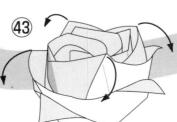

Curl the outside petals.

Curl the middle petals.

FOUR LEAVES (P2)

Four corners of paper turn out four leaves. Make creases in advance and fold all at once.

ROSE LEAVES (P2)

Fold one of **the Four Leaves** into a strip and make a stem. Insert it into the space at the bottom of the rose flower.

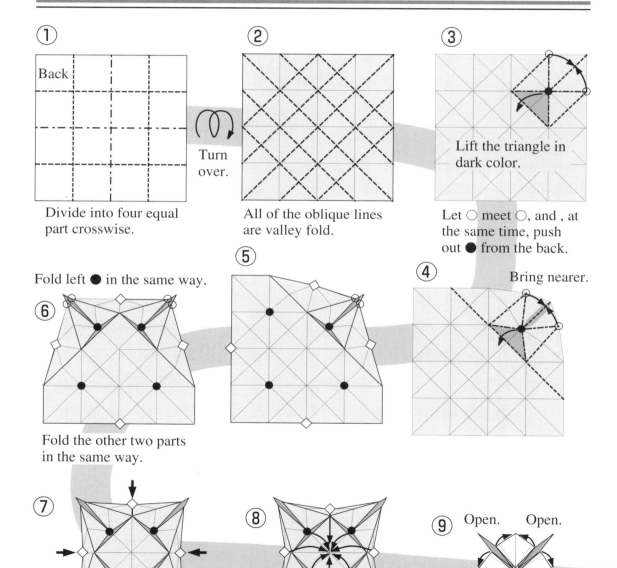

① Back

Divide into four equal part crosswise.

Turn over.

② All of the oblique lines are valley fold.

③ Lift the triangle in dark color.

Let ○ meet ○, and , at the same time, push out ● from the back.

④ Bring nearer.

Fold left ● in the same way.

⑤

⑥ Fold the other two parts in the same way.

⑦

⑧ Bring eight tips all together to the center.

⑨ Open. Open.

Open. Open.

Part Ⅱ Rose

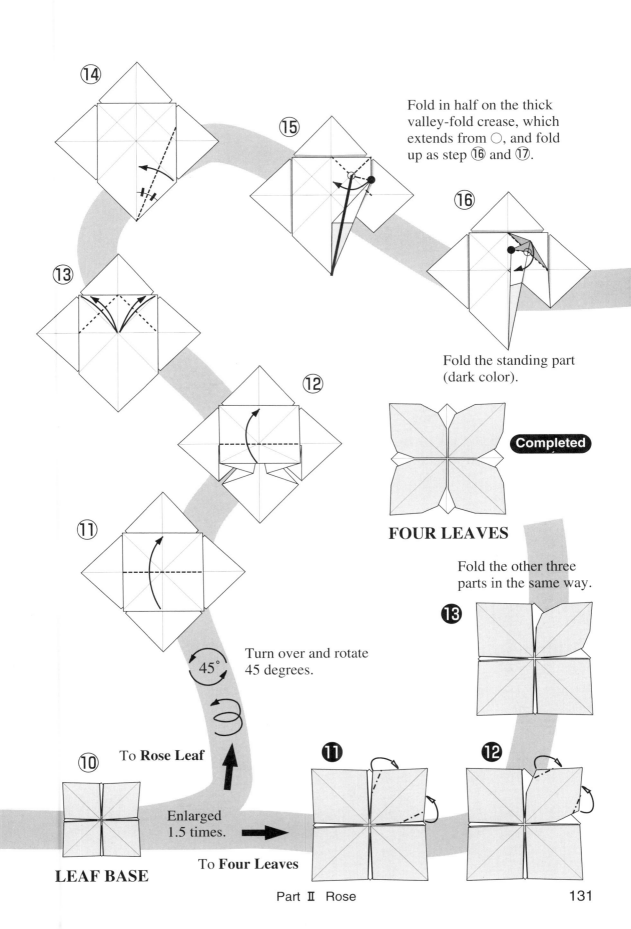

⑭

⑮

Fold in half on the thick valley-fold crease, which extends from ○, and fold up as step ⑯ and ⑰.

⑯

⑬

Fold the standing part (dark color).

Completed

FOUR LEAVES

⑫

Fold the other three parts in the same way.

⓭

⑪

Turn over and rotate 45 degrees.

45°

⓫

⓬

⑩

To **Rose Leaf**

Enlarged 1.5 times.

LEAF BASE

To **Four Leaves**

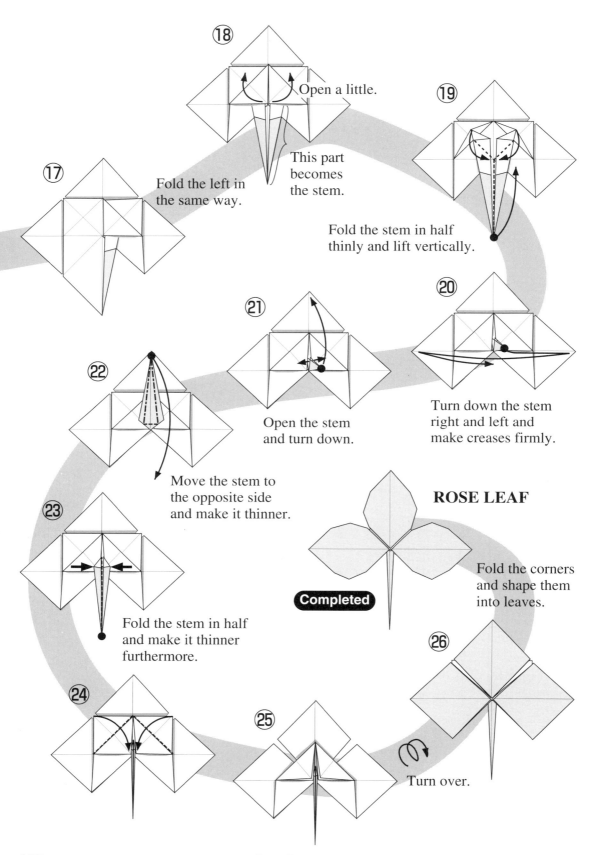

⑱ Open a little.

This part becomes the stem.

⑰ Fold the left in the same way.

⑲ Fold the stem in half thinly and lift vertically.

⑳ Turn down the stem right and left and make creases firmly.

㉑ Open the stem and turn down.

㉒ Move the stem to the opposite side and make it thinner.

㉓ Fold the stem in half and make it thinner furthermore.

ROSE LEAF

Fold the corners and shape them into leaves.

Completed

㉖

㉔

㉕ Turn over.

PYRAMID

(Rectangular paper: $1 : \sqrt{2}$)

Let's make a tall pyramid which suggests the one in Rome. There are lots of pyramids like this in Europe. The pyramid designed on the U.S. dollar note is of the same shape. Use ordinary oblong paper from a notebook. If you fold acetate film, you can use it as a case. You may also fold an OHP sheet, but it is thick and you will have to fold many times, pressing your fingers against the sheet with force.

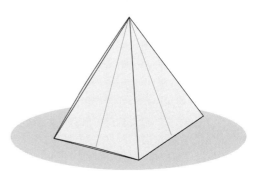

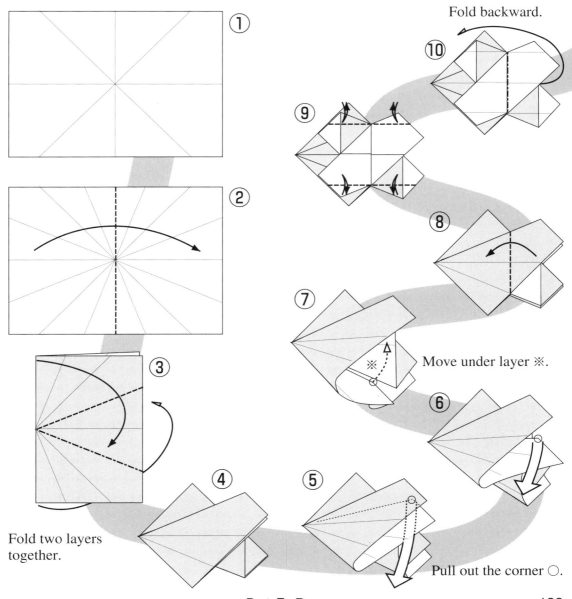

Fold backward.

Move under layer ※.

Pull out the corner ○.

Fold two layers together.

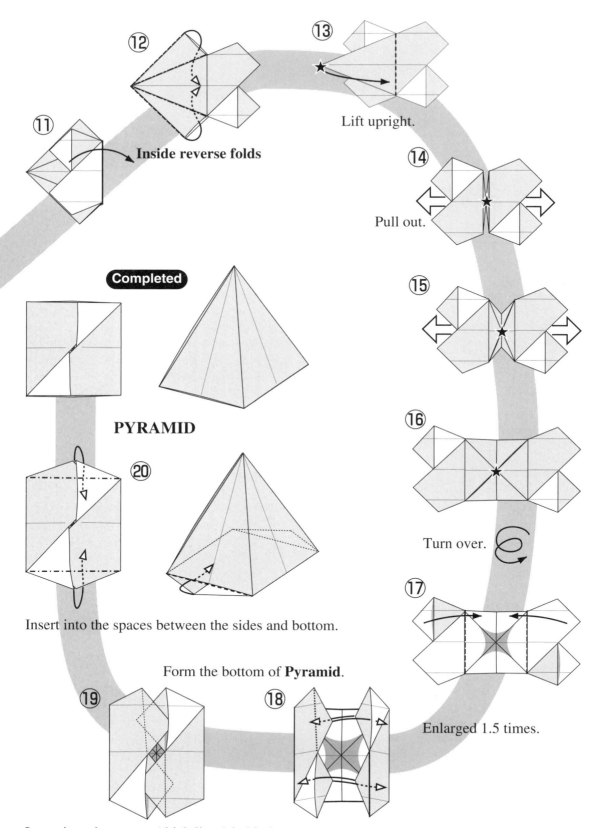

⑪ Inside reverse folds

⑫

⑬ Lift upright.

⑭ Pull out.

⑮

⑯ Turn over.

⑰ Enlarged 1.5 times.

Completed

PYRAMID

⑳ Insert into the spaces between the sides and bottom.

Form the bottom of **Pyramid**.

⑲ Insert into the spaces (thick lines) behind.

⑱

Part II Rose

Part III
The Geometry of Origami

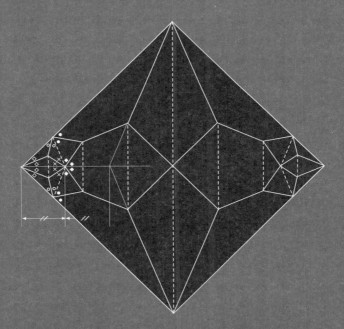

Preamble
Flat Folding Condition
Mountain-fold Crease and Valley-fold Crease
The Geometry of Orizuru

Chapter 1 Preamble

1.1 The International Meeting of Origami Science

So far the International Meeting of Origami Science has been held twice. The first meeting was held in December in 1989 in Ferrara in north central Italy. It was planned and organized by Humiaki Huzita alone. He was Professor at the Patova University, which is well-known for Galileo Galilei who taught there. The results of the meeting were collected and published in book form under the title "Origami Science and Technology". The size of the book is about 7" by 10" and it has 392 pages. It contains studies of mathematics and engineering related to origami as well as the minutes of the meeting. The second meeting was held in November in 1994 in Ohtsu City in Shiga Prefecture. The subjects discussed at the meeting covered science of form, education, art, and history besides mathematics and engineering in the first meeting.

They were published under the title of "Origami Science and Art" in the format of 7" by 10" with 555 pages.

In this way, origami science is growing and the information and ideas are internationally exchanged, but **geometry of Origami** is little known by the public. Therefore, the basis and its application (**geometry of Orizuru**) are introduced here.

1.2 Development Chart

Geometry of origami is a study to investigate the mathematical characteristics which origami has. However, it is very difficult to study origami itself that is folded.

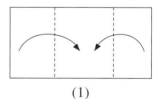

(1)

Example 1.1 Figure 1 (1) shows how to fold **Door Base**. There is only one diagram of creases, but we have two folding (2) and (3) for (1). In origami, we usually fold many times, so the number of folds increases suddenly and it becomes very difficult to grasp all folding. The object of the study, therefore, is narrowed down to the creases on plain paper instead of the work itself.

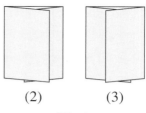

(2) (3)

Fig.1

Figure 2 shows a catamaran and its **development chart** (crease chart). Broken lines are **valley-fold creases** and chain lines with dots are **mountain-fold creases**. The creases, which appear only in the process, are excluded from the development chart. The chart such as that of the catamaran is simple, but it is hard to distinguish the broken lines from the chain lines with dots, so in this book the mountain-fold creases are shown in solid lines as far as there is no fear of confusion.

It is hard to imagine the completed form from the development chart, but you can roughly understand the structure. Figure 2 (2) is symmetrical. The symmetry of the figure suggests the catamaran. Figure 3 is the development chart of a well-known origami. Can you guess what is the original origami? I will give a hint. The corners where creases focus become thin when folded. The answer is in Section 1 of Chapter 4.

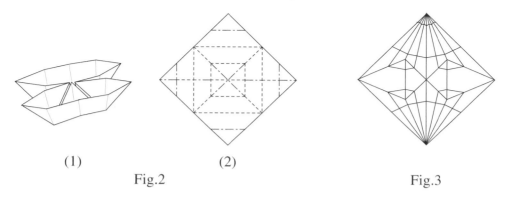

(1)   (2)

Fig.2   Fig.3

Figure 4 (1) is a cube of balloon neatly folded and (2) is its development chart. There is one problem. Unlike the catamaran, the creases that make the sides of the cube are half-open. Origami artist, Kunihiko Kasahara called this **'hankai-ori (3D-fold)'**. In order to show the 3D-fold in the development chart, we have to add each angle. The 3D-fold makes the chart more complicated than the flat fold which only discriminates the mountain and valley folds. Figure 5 shows folding along the curve. Not only the fold line makes a curve, but also the angles between the flat surface and the curved surface differ depending on the positions. It is more complicated than the 3D-fold. How can we handle this problem? It is too difficult, so we have to postpone dealing with the problem. For this reason, we will limit the scope of our study to the flat fold, that is folding paper on a flat plane, in this book.

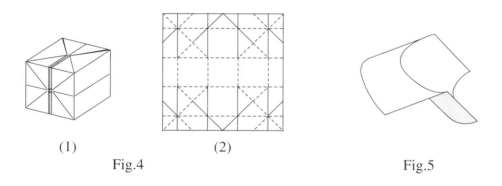

(1)   (2)

Fig.4   Fig.5

Chapter 2 Flat Folding Condition

2.1 Bisection Fold of an Angle and the Inner Center of a Triangle

Fold a triangle ABC by aligning side AB with side BC (Figure 6 (1)). When opened like (2), the overlapping angles are equal, so the crease is a bisector of angle B. This fold is called **bisection fold of an angle**, including the mountain fold.

Next make the bisection fold at the three corners at the same time. The three valley-fold creases meet at one point, which is an intersection point of bisectors, as shown in Figure 7. This point is **the inner center** of the triangle. If the triangle is folded flat a new mountain-fold crease is made like Figure 8. Figure 9 is the development chart. The bisection fold of an angle is technically a method of overlapping sides, so the three sides AB, CD and AD overlap side BC as shown in Figure 8. As a result, side AD overlaps side CD. This means that mountain-fold crease ID in Figure 9 is a perpendicular drawn toward side AC. There are two other perpendiculars which are drawn from the inner center I, and it is possible to flatten the triangle by making mountain fold on these in place of ID. These three perpendiculars function as a hinge (Figure 10).

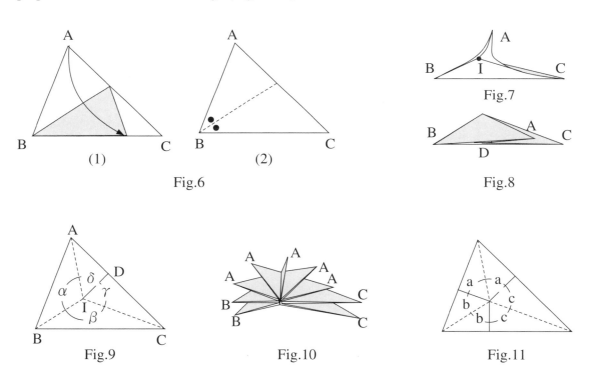

Fig.6

Fig.7

Fig.8

Fig.9

Fig.10

Fig.11

2.2 Husimi's Theorem

If you add two perpendiculars to Figure 9, it becomes Figure 11. Each triangle across the broken lines is congruent, so three bisectors are produced. In reference to Figure 9, an important equation, **Husimi's theorem** is obtained.

(i) $\alpha + \gamma = \beta + \delta = 180°$

Crumple a piece of paper up into a ball, flatten and open. You can get a development chart with random creases. Measure the angles where four creases meet with a protractor. Then the sum of alternate angles around a vertex formed by those folds will equal 180 degrees, allowing marginal errors by the thickness of paper.

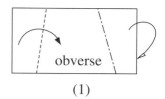

(1)

2.3 Locally Flat Folding Condition

Let's consider an example which has more than five creases. The result is definite as Husimi's theorem.

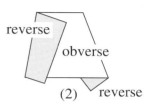

(2)

Fig.12

Theorem 1   When flat folding is possible on creases which extend radially from one point,
(i) the number of fold lines is even and it is more than four.
(ii) the sum of alternate angles around the vertex is 180 degrees.

Proof of (i)   The obverse and reverse of the paper folded on the crease becomes opposite, irrespective of mountain or valley folds (Figure 12). Let's assume that the number of the fold lines is odd and write 'obverse' and 'reverse' alternately in the developing chart. Then, there appears a part where adjacent faces are the same like Figure 13. It is contradiction. Therefore the number of fold lines must be even.

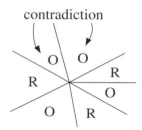

O: obverse
R: reverse

Fig.13

Proof of (ii)   Now give you an example of six fold lines (Figure 14 (1)). The (2) shows folded form. Imagine that an ant walks along the arc. Make O the starting point and indicate the positions of the ant along the circumference. At the point A, the position is a, and at the point B, the position is a-b, and so on. The ant makes a round and returns to point O. The trace of the ant is a $-b+c-d+e-f$. The sum shows point O :therefore a $-b+c-d+e-f=0$, that is, $a+c+e=b+d+f$.

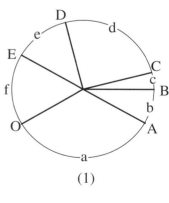

(1)

The length of arc is proportional to the central angle, so the sum of alternate central angles are the same. The sum of the central angles is 360 degrees. Therefore the half is 180 degrees. For more fold lines, the theorem will be proved in the same way. The proof is concluded. Condition (ii) of main theorem 1 is called **Locally Flat Folding Condition**.

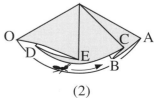

(2)

Fig.14

Chapter 3   Mountain-fold Crease and Valley-fold Crease

3.1 Mountain Fold and Valley Fold

Figure 15 shows **valley fold** and **mountain fold**. The valley-fold crease is given in broken lines, and mountain-fold crease in chain lines with dots (in solid lines for copmlex figure).

Figure 17 is the development charts of figure 16. The folds (mountain or valley) are different, but the connections and angles are the same. Therefore, we will call the development chart, which shows all creases in solid lines, **formal crease chart**. Setting aside the development chart, the plane divided by segments, half lines and straight lines are called **cell decomposition**. From theorem 1,
(i) Formal crease chart $\Rightarrow$ Cell decomposition which satisfies the locally flat folding condition at each vertex.

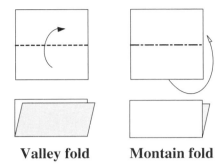

Valley fold   **Montain fold**

Fig.15

Fig.16

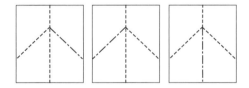

Fig.17

3.2 Real Mountain-Valley System

Figure 18 is a formal crease chart. There are 16 ways to give four lines mountain-valley folds ($2^4 = 16$), but actually only four ways are possible (Figure 19).

Definition 3.1   Regardless of actual folds, the mountain-valley folds given to the lines in the formal crease chart K is called **the formal mountain-valley system** and denoted by $C(K)$. A formal mountain-valley system is called a real **real mountain-valley system**, if it is actually folded.

The formal mountain-valley system of the formal crease chart, which is composed of n lines, has 2^n variations. The theme of Chapter 3 is selecting real mountain-valley systems from formal mountain-valley systems. In the case of a simple example, it is easy to find out whether the formal crease chart has a real mountain-valley system or not by folding paper actually. But there is a case when it is impossible to fold no matter how you may try.

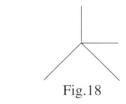

Fig.18

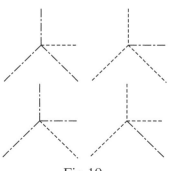

Fig.19

Is the method wrong or is it absolutely impossible? Try your hand by the formal crease chart of Figure 20.

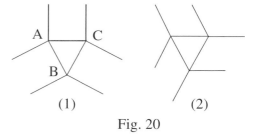

Fig. 20

3.3 Adjacent Mountain-Valley Crease Condition

Generally it is very difficult to deal with the real mountain-valley system of the formal crease chart, so it will be better to start with simple cases. The simplest formal crease chart is the one which has only one vertex, that is the chart which consists of the lines that radiate from one point. We should think that the formal crease chart is decomposition of the whole plane, but to make the matter simpler, I will explain it using the examples of cut-out square or circle. The circle is cut out with the center placed on the vertex in the case of one vertex .

Proposition 3.1 When folding a sector on the two lines extending from its center,
(i) if $\beta < \alpha$ and $\beta < \gamma$, then the mountain and valley of the two fold lines are opposite.

Proof If you try to make valley folds on the two lines, the two flaps clash like Figure 21 (2) and you are unable to fold flat. If you make mountain folds, the result will be the same. Therefore you have to make a mountain fold on one line and a valley fold on the other as shown in (3). QED. Condition (i) is called the **adjacent mountain-valley creases condition**.

Caution: If $\beta = \alpha$ or $\beta = \gamma$ in (i), the two fold lines will be unrelated. If you fold the sector of the same size as β on β, the remaining sector can be folded on either sides.

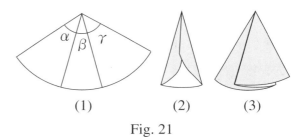

Fig. 21

Theorem 2 In the real mountain-valley system of the formal crease chart, which has only one vertex,
(ii) the difference of the number of mountain-fold lines and valley-fold lines $= 2$.

Proof If you cut the folded circle horizontally, you can obtain closed snapped lines like Figure 22 (1)-(3). If

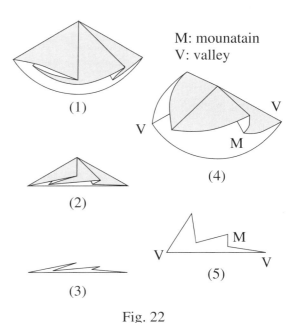

M: mounatain
V: valley

Fig. 22

The sum of the interior angles of the closed snapped line (polygon) is [{fold lines} −2]× 180°, The value is unrelated with the sizes of folds. However, the size of each interior angle varies in accordance with the fold, and the mountain-fold line finally comes to 360° and the valley fold line to 0°. The sum of the interior angles is mountain-fold lines×360° and we can derive the following equations: {mountain-fold lines}×360°={fold lines−2} ×180°and {mountain-fold lines}={fold lines}/2−1.

When combined with {mountain-fold lines}+{valley-fold lines}={fold lines}, {valley-fold lines}={mountain-fold lines}+2.
When the back of paper is mirrored,
the mountain-valley is reversed and
{mountain-fold lines}={valley-fold lines}+2
and (ii) is obtained. QED.

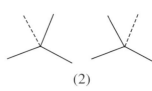

(1)   (2)

Fig.23

Proposition 3.2 The real mountain-valley system of the formal crease chart ($\delta < \alpha \leqq \gamma < \beta$) like Figure 23 (1) has only four kinds as shown in (2).
Proof As stated in the adjacent mountain-valley crease condition of proposition 3.1, the mountain and valley of the two lines, which sandwich angle δ , are opposite. According to theorem 2 (ii), the other two lines must be either a mountain fold or a valley fold. Therefore the only four kinds of (2) are possible. QED.
Caution: In the inequality of proposition 3.2, if $\delta = \alpha$ and $\gamma = \beta$, the number of the real mountain-valley systems increases more, because the constraint of the adjacent mountain-valley fold lines reduces. It will become easier to understand proposition 3.2, if it is expressed as follows.
Proposition 3.3 In the real mountain-valley system of the formal crease chart ($\delta < \alpha \leqq \gamma < \beta$) in Proposition 3.2,
(iii) the mountain-valley of the adjacent fold lines of a narrow angle is opposite, and
(iv) the mountain-valley of the adjacent fold lines of a wide angle is the same.

It was impossible to fold flat the formal crease chart in Figure 20 (1). The reason can be explained by this proposition as follows; We assume that AB is a valley-fold line and apply Proposition 3.3 to each vertex A and B, then find that AC and BC become mountain-fold lines. And if applied to vertex B, BC becomes a valley-fold line. This is contradictory. Therefore we cannot fold the chart flat. (There exists no real mountain-valley system.)

3.4 Existence Theorem of Real Local Mountain-Valley System

Proposition 3.3 and Main Theorem 2 are simple, but they are important propositions which are applied to all cases. There is another important proposition with regard to local structures.

Theorem 3 (Existence Theorem of Real Local Mountain-Valley System)
There exist, at least, two real mountain-valley systems in the formal crease chart which has only one vertex.

Proof The explanation is given using formal crease chart of Figure 24 (1). First make a cut in one of the fold lines. Next fold the lines in numerical order like (2), valley, mountain, valley and the like alternately. The separated lines align like (3), which is guaranteed by the locally flat folding condition, and they can be joined together like (4). This folded form gives an example of the real mountain-valley system of K. If all the mountain and valley folds are reversed, another real mountain-valley system is obtained. Depending on the line to be cut, a flap comes between Face e and Face s and they cannot be joined like (6). In that case, redo by making a cut in the fold line, which comes to the edge in (6). QED.

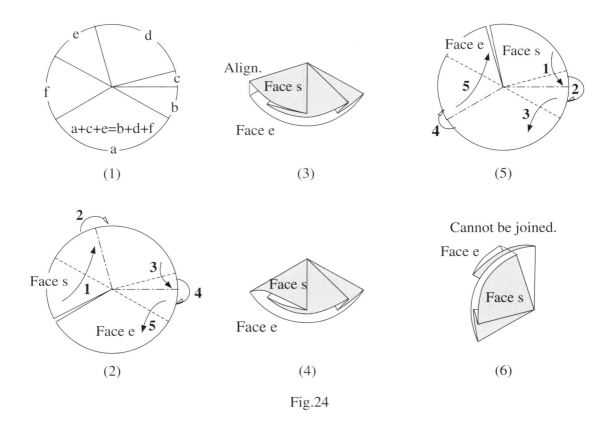

Fig.24

3.5 In the case of Two Vertexes

Let's examine the real mountain-valley system of formal crease chart of Figure 25. There are three areas δ, γ, and ρ. Figure 26 (1) and (2) show the three areas cut out. In the case of (1), you can fold the δ and ρ either ways, forward or backward. In (2), however, each δ and ρ must be folded toward opposite sides alternately. In other words,
 (i) the mountain and valley of the two fold lines are opposite.

This is the same as Proposition 3.1 (i). Shapes (1) and (2) are produced from the same formal crease chart, but why is the result different? In principle, the formal crease chart should be examined on the plane as a whole. To cut out part of the plane is temporary measures. The larger (2) is rather near the real nature. The reason why the constraint (i) is not applied to (1) is that the cut-out area is small and the δ and ρ didn't happen to clash with each other.

Figure 27 (1) is Figure 26 (1) with narrow γ. To fold δ and ρ on the same side, you have to tear the paper as (2) and it is subject to constraint (i). This can be construed as follows: Figure 27 (1) is Figure 26 (2) viewed from a distance. They are identical, so it is natural that they are not free from constraint (i).

In formal crease charts of Figure 28 (1), (2) and (3), if you fold δ and ρ regardless of mountain and valley folds, they move to the gray parts. In (1) and (2), the folded parts overlap as (4) and (5), so they cannot be folded on the same side. But (3) does not overlap as (6), so you can make mountain and valley folds as desired. Why does (3) differ from others?

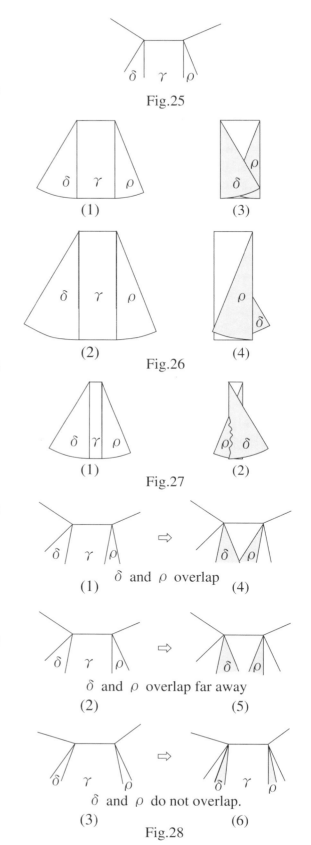

Fig.25

(1)

(3)

(2)

(4)

Fig.26

(1)

(2)

Fig.27

(1)

δ and ρ overlap

(4)

(2)

δ and ρ overlap far away

(5)

(3)

δ and ρ do not overlap.

(6)

Fig.28

If you view Figure 28 (3) from a distance, it looks like Figure 29. Macroscopically, it is identical with the formal crease chart with one vertex like Figure 29 (3). {The central angle of γ of Figure 29 (3)} = {the sum of the two interior angles of γ of (1)} $-180°$. Therefore if this angle is smaller than the interior angles of adjacent δ and ρ, it is under constraint (i) by Proposition 3.1. Thus,

Definition 3.2 We let K be a formal crease chart with two vertexes (A and B) as shown in Figure 30 (1). The cell decomposition (2) where the lines meet jointly on vertex A is called **localization of K on A** and denoted by K_A. And the chart where lines AB meet on one vertex is called **AB compression of K** and denoted by K/AB.

Proposition 3.4 If the K is the formal crease chart of Definition 3.3, K_A, K_B, and K/AB are formal crease charts.

Proof It is obvious that K_A and K_B are formal crease charts. If each angle of fold lines is designated as in Figure 31 (1), angles λ and μ in the compression K/AB are
$\lambda = \alpha_1 + \beta_1 - 180$,
$\mu = \alpha_m + \beta_n - 180$ and
the sum of the alternate angles in K/AB
$= \lambda + \alpha_3 + ... + \alpha_{m-1} + \beta_{n-1} + ... + \beta_3$
$= \alpha_1 + \beta_1 - 180 + \alpha_3 + ... + \alpha_{m-1} + \beta_{n-1}$
$\quad + ... + \beta_3$
$= (\alpha_1 + \alpha_3 + ... + \alpha_{m-1}) + (\beta_{n-1} + ... + \beta_3 + \beta_1) - 180$
$= 180$
This satisfies the locally flat folding condition and the compression K/AB is a formal crease chart.

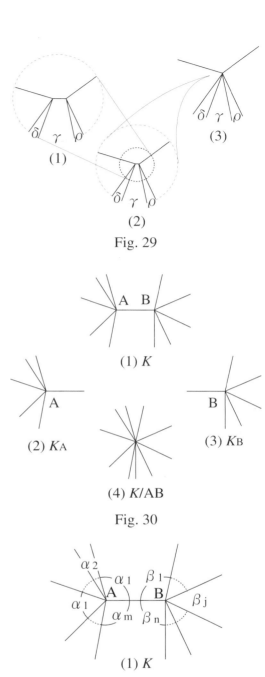

Fig. 29

Fig. 30

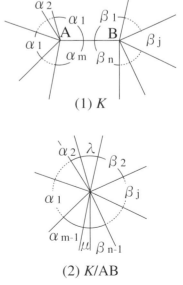

Fig. 31

Caution: In the case of $\lambda = 0$ or $\mu = 0$. the lines overlap by compression AB, and they disappear as in Figure 32.

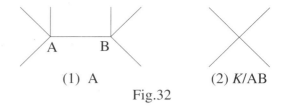

(1) A   (2) K/AB

Fig.32

Definition 3.3   In regard to the formal crease chart K and its formal mountain-valley system C(K) of Definition 3.2, the KA and K/AB, on which the mountain-valley folds are made according to the mountain valley of C(K), are called **localization of C(K) on A and AB compression of C(K)** respectively and expressed as **C(K)A**, and **C(K)/AB**.

Theorem 4   If the K is the formal crease chart of Definition 3.2, the following is true. The formal mountain-valley system C(K) of K is a real mountain-valley system ⇔ C(K)A, C(K)B, C(K)/AB are real mountain-valley systems of KA, KB and K/AB, respectively.

Proof of (⇒):   Fold the K according to C(K) and cut out the part near vertex A, which is KA. The mountain-valley of KA is the same as that of C(K). Therefore C(K)A is the real mountain-valley system of KA (Figure 3.3 (1)-(5)). The same applies to C(K)B.

Now reduce the width of the belt area of (6) little by little until it is completely curtailed. This corresponds to (1) of Figure 29 viewed from a distance. If viewed from an infinite point, A and B look overlapped like (8). This is a folded form of K/AB. The mountain valley fold lines of (1) and (8) are identical, so C(K)/AB becomes the real mountain-valley system of K/AB. The (7) and (9) are development charts of (6) and (8).

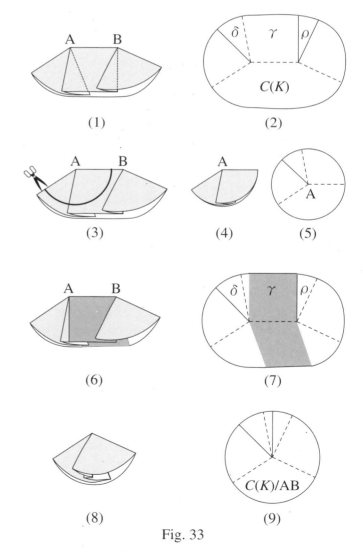

Fig. 33

If the fold lines which run on both sides of area γ are parallel, the whole γ is reduced when compressed as shown in Figure 34. In (2), area σ and area ρ are pasted up into one, and it is consistent with the disappearance of fold lines as cautioned in Proposition 3.4.

Proof of ($\Leftarrow$)   Prepare two $C(K)$'s. Cut off Figure 35(1) on thick lines and separate it into (3) and (4). It is assumed that $C(K)_A$ and $C(K)_B$ are real mountain-valley systems of K_A and K_B, so (3) and (4) can be folded. If the gray area of (1) is overlapped and pasted up, the fold of $C(K)$ can be obtained. QED.

Caution: It seems that the assumption that $C(K)$/AB is the real mountain-valley system of K/AB is not used in the proof of ($\Leftarrow$). But without this condition, the following inconsistent result would be produced.

Example 3.1   In the formal mountain-valley system $C(K)$ in Figure 36 (1), localization K_A and K_B are real mountain-valley systems, but the compression $C(K)$/AB of (2) is not. The reason is that in the localized folds (3) and (4), which are folded in the same way as in Figure 33, the gray areas cannot be overlapped, because the parts marked ※ will collide. If the two points A and B draw near, the collision will occur near the vertex. If the two points overlap into one, the K/AB can be folded and others will go smoothly. Incidentally, the (5), which is obtained by separating (2), cannot be pasted up as shown in (6).

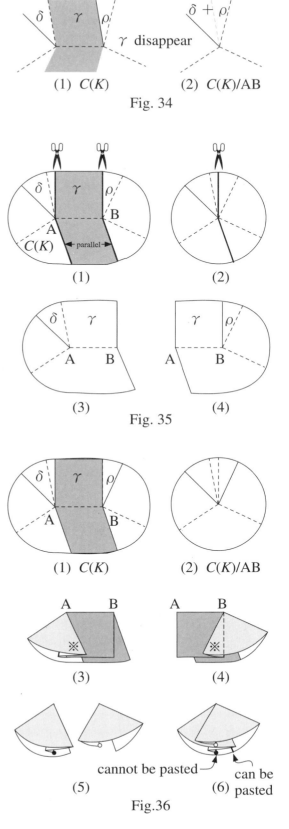

(1) $C(K)$ (2) $C(K)$/AB

Fig. 34

(1)   (2)

(3)   (4)

Fig. 35

(1) $C(K)$ (2) $C(K)$/AB

(3)   (4)

cannot be pasted —   can be
(5)   (6) pasted

Fig.36

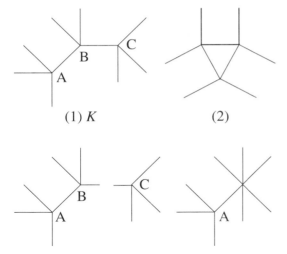

(1) K (2)

(3) *K*AB and *K*C (4) *K*AB

Fig.37

3.6 The Base of Mountain-Valley System

Main theorem 4 can be applied to three vertexes like Figure 37 (1), because it is considered in the same way as those which have less than two vertexes as localized *K*AB and *K*C in (3) and compression *K*/BC in (4). On the other hand, Main theorem 4 cannot be applied to (2), because all the compressed lines disappear. Is it necessary to fold actually to investigate the mountain-valley of (2)? It has been proved in section 3 that the (2) has no real mountain-valley system by making use of Proposition 3.3, that is, the mountain-valley fold lines AB, BC and CA are interfering with each other. Thus,

Definition 3.4 In the formal crease chart K, when mountain-valley is given to fold lines ℓ, the lines, of which mountain-valley is uniquely decided according to Proposition 3.3, are expressed as [ℓ] and it is called **The base of mountain-valley system *K* belonging to** ℓ.

Example 3.2 The bases of the formal crease chart of Figure 38 (1) are [ℓ] and [m] of (2). Each of them has two kinds of mountain-valley respectively as shown in (3). Figure 39 (1) is one of the real mountain-valley systems of Figure 38 (1), and if it is folded it becomes (2). If this is re-folded as in steps (2)-(6), you can obtain real mountain-valley system (7). This transformation corresponds to the manipulation to reverse the mountain-valley of base [ℓ].

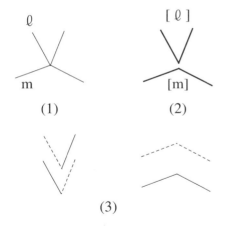

(1) (2)

(3)

Fig.38

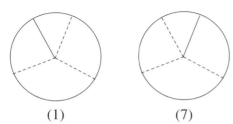

(1) (7)

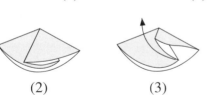

(2) (3)

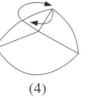

(4)

(5)

(6)

Fig.39

Example 3.3 Figure 40 (1) and (2) are a formal crease chart and its real mountain-valley system. If it is folded, it becomes (3) (cf. References [F], [Mo]). This is called a **twisted fold**. The (1) has four bases like (4). If you reverse the mountain-valley of thick lines in (2) and fold (5), you can obtain (6). This change of mountain-valley corresponds to the turning over of pocket (re-fold of ※ of (3)).l

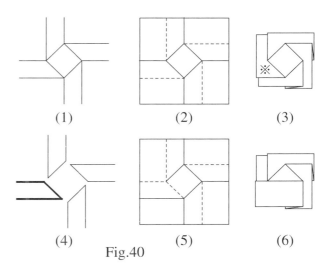

Fig.40

3.7 The Role of Base

The base is an important conception to connect localized mountain-valley structures.

Example 3.4 Figure 41 is a chart which was found out when searching regular formal crease charts by using a computer. The thick lines of (1) are closed bases, but there are no real mountain-valley system since they contain contradiction like (2). In other words, they cannot be folded flat no matter how mountain-valley folds are made.

Example 3.5 The bases of the formal crease chart of Figure 42 (1) are sides of isosceles trapezoids such as S and T (thick lines). They are expressed as [S] and [T]. These bases have two kinds of mountain-valley as shown in (2). If you actually fold them, you will find that they are real mountain-valley systems regardless of their positions. Namely, the bases are independent.

Those that have regular structure of fold lines as this example are called **'hiraori'**. Mathematically, two-dimensional crystal group is functioning, so we may call it an invariable origami, but I call it **crystallographic origami** including solid forms. Figure 43 (2) is hiraori, which is well known as **brick folding**. The (1) is its development chart. Figure 44 is also hiraori and the bases are all parallelograms. See biography [F] for details about hiraori.

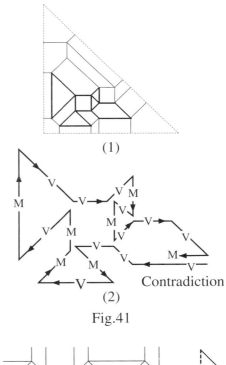

Fig.41

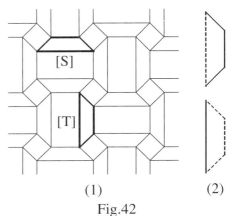

Fig.42

3.8 The Difficulty in Dealing with Bases

Example 3.6 Figure 45 (1) is part of Figure 42 (1). To put it more precisely, it is localization of trapezoid T. It has four bases as shown in (2). In Example 3.5, the bases were independent, but those of Figure 45 (2), [ℓ] and [m] are not, because the mountain-valley of ℓ and m must be reversed according to Main theorem 4.

If the formal central angle of area γ is defined using compression like angle λ of Proposition 3.4, it becomes 0. Including this kind of angle, it is possible to prove that Proposition 3.3 is true. If the bases are redefined by expanded Proposition 3.3, [ℓ] and [m] are linked into one, and they become a large base like (3). In this way, we know that there are four kinds of the real mountain-valley system of (1), (4) and (5) and their reversions.

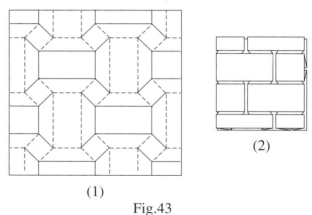

(1)

(2)

Fig.43

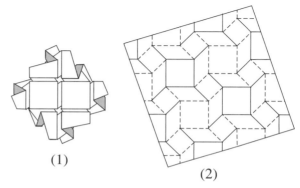

(1)

(2)

Fig.44

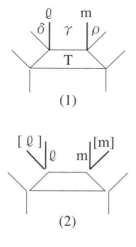

(1)

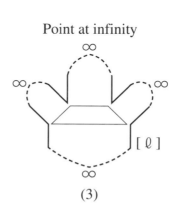

Point at infinity

(3)

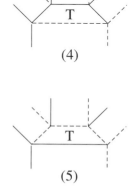

(4)

(5)

Fig.45

Example 3.7 If the lines of Figure 42 (1) are lengthened, Figure 46 (1) is obtained. If you try to fold bases [S] and [T] like (2), the two trapezoids collide and you cannot fold. Accordingly, you have to fold in opposite directions with the rectangle in between. In other words, [S] and [T] are not independent. This applies to all the trapezoids that are congruent with S.

Suppose that there is a part, which was folded by a real mountain valley system, in Figure 46 (1). Let the part be base [T]. If you try to reverse the mountain-valley of base [T], it affects other parts. And you will be obliged to reverse the mountain-valley of not only S, but also all the trapezoids, which are congruent with S. The non-independence of the base like this is essentially the same as Example 3.6. We should understand that the base of Example 3.5 was independent, because the width of the area happened to be small. In other words, we must construe that

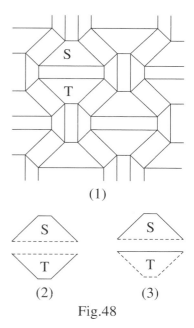

(1)

(2)   (3)

Fig.48

(i) the base shows the minimum limits on which the mountain-valley of fold lines interdependent

(ii) there is always interdependence between bases.

The (i) and (ii) seem to have something in common with the relations of states in the world. Don't you think so?

3.9 The Normal Vertex and the Singular Vertex

Lastly, I will explain another cause that makes the mountain-valley problem difficult.

Example 3.8 In Figure 47, white dots means 90° and black dots 45°. All the devices to solve the mountain-valley problems are based on Proposition 3.1, but it is valid as long as the adjacent three angles are not equal. Accordingly, if the adjacent angles are equal as in Figure 47, the results in this chapter cannot be obtained. And the following definition:

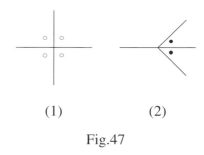

(1)   (2)

Fig.47

Definition 3.5 In the formal crease chart, if the angles of the adjacent fold lines are not equal, the vertex is called as the **Normal Vertex**, and the vertex that is not Normal Vertex the **Singular Vertex**.

In regard to the mountain-valley problems of the formal crease chart with a singular vertex, nothing has been known about the general theory.

Chapter 4   The Geometry of Orizuru

4.1 Husimi's Generalized of Bird Base

Most origami is folded from colored square paper. Its representatives are a yakko (serving man) and an orizuru (crane).

But it is possible to fold the orizuru from paper other than a square. If you fold along the creases made in rhombic paper like Figure 48 (1), you can make an orizuru with long wings. Many people have been aware the fact from old times. However, you cannot make a beautiful orizuru from a rectangular.

The quadrilateral, of which lines are symmetrical with respect to a diagonal line, is called the **kite shape** (Figure 48 (2)). Kohji Husimi thought of folding an orizuru from kite-shape paper when he was working on a flying orizuru. The details will be explained later, but it is not simple and easy to fold the orizuru from kite-shape paper. To find out the method, the help of mathematics is necessary after repeated trial and error.

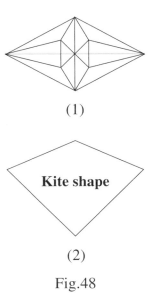

(1)

Kite shape

(2)

Fig.48

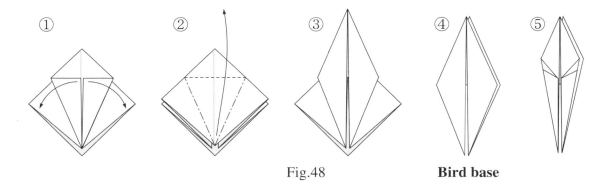

Fig.48   **Bird base**

Figure 49 shows part of the folding process of an ordinary orizuru. The ④ is the **Bird Base**, which is often employed when making birds. The lower half of ④ is folded in half into slender forms and they become a neck and a tail (legs) when folded up between wings. Figure 50 (1) and (2) are development charts of the bird base of orizuru respectively. In those charts, the central point, where six fold lines meet, becomes the center of the back of orizuru, and it is called a **bird-base center**.

4.2 The Failure of Natural Deformation and Maekawa's Deformation

The deformation of orizuru is possible by changing the shape of paper, but it is also possible by destroying the symmetry. Figure 51 illustrates the method, but actually, it is impossible to fold the orizuru by this method. It is good up to ④ before making the neck and tail slender, but the part folded inward (dotted lines of ④) gets caught and the neck and tail cannot be raised. Admitting the failure, try to fold according to the processes of Figure 51, you will understand the meaning of getting caught.

Jun Maekawa, who is known by his masterpiece **'Devil'** and his **geometrical origami design**, worked out the solution to the catch in his **'Maekawa's New Orizuru'** (bibliographies [Kasa]). Figure 52 is the method. After ③ is almost the same as the ordinary folding of the orizuru. It is also possible to make a symmetrical wings by Maekawa's deformation.

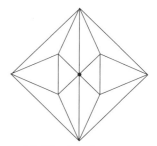

(1) The development chart of the bird base

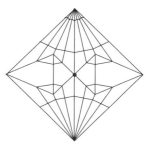

(2) The development chart of the orizuru

Fig. 50

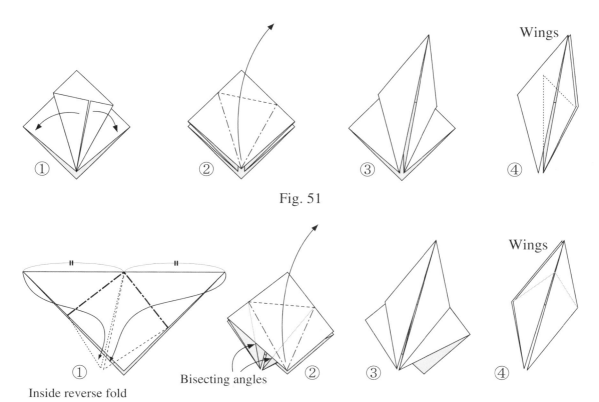

Fig. 51

Inside reverse fold

Bisecting angles

Fig.52 Maekawa's deformation

4.3 The Quadrilateral with the Inscribed Circle

A circle circumscribed by a polygon is called the **inscribed circle** (Figure 53 (1)). In this section, an interesting feature of a quadrilateral, which has the inscribed circle, is dealt with. The bisection fold of the angle, which was explained in Chapter 2, also applies to quadrilaterals. Unlike the case of a triangle, however, the bisection fold of the angle cannot be applied to all the quadrilaterals. It can be applied only to special quadrilaterals. Those quadrilaterals have an inscribed circle and are closely related with the deformation of orizuru.

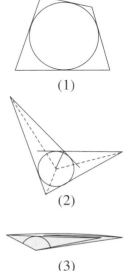

(1)

(2)

(3)

Fig. 53

Definition 4.1 When you can fold a quadrilateral flat by bisectors of the four corners, this fold can be called **bisection fold of a quadrilateral**.

Proposition 4.1 The necessary and sufficient condition for quadrilateral ABCD to be folded on the bisector of the angle is that it has an inscribed circle. However, when the quadrilateral has a reentrant angle, the inscribed circle and reentrant sides are tangent on their extension lines (Figure 53).

Proof of the necessary condition: According to Definition 4.1, fold lines or bisectors of the angle intersect at a point. We name this point I in Figure 54 (1). The two sides bisected by a fold line overlap, so the four sides of the quadrilateral overlap on the same straight line (Figure 54 (2)). On the folded form, if you draw a circle round central point I, it is tangent to the four sides when opened. Namely, it is an inscribed circle.

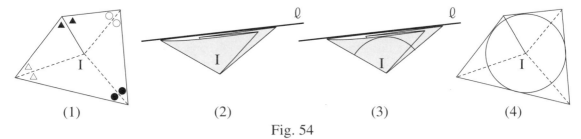

(1)　　　　(2)　　　　(3)　　　　(4)

Fig. 54

Proof of the sufficient condition: If you draw perpendicular lines toward the four sides from central point I of the inscribed circle, you obtain four groups of triangles which have oblique sides jointly. The perpendicular lines are radii of the inscribed circle, so they are all equal in length. Accordingly, the triangles of each group are congruent, and each oblique side is a bisector.

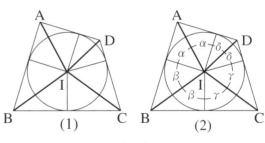

Fig. 55

Moreover, in Figure 55(2), $\angle AIB + \angle CID = (\alpha + \beta) + (\gamma + \delta) = (\alpha + \delta) + (\beta + \gamma)$ $= \angle AID + \angle BID$ and $2(\alpha + \beta + \gamma + \delta) = 360°$ and $\angle AIB + \angle CID = \angle AID + \angle BIC$ $= 180°$. Therefore, four lines IA, IB, IC, ID satisfies the locally flat folding condition, and it is possible to fold quadrilateral ABCD on the bisector of the angle. QED.

Proposition 4.2 The necessary and sufficient condition for quadrilateral ABCD to have an inscribed circle is
(i) AB + CD = BC + DA

Proof of the necessary condition of (i): Figure 56 (1) is a quadrilateral with an inscribed circle. If you draw lines from the center of the circle toward the points of contact, you will obtain four groups of right triangles, and AB + CD = (p+q) + (s+t) = (q+s) + (t+p) = BC + DA

Proof of the sufficient condition of (i): Draw a circle which comes in contact with three sides as Figure 57 and make the radius r. If you draw perpendicular lines from the center of the circle toward the four sides, by the Pythagorean theorem,
(ii) $x^2 + y^2 = ID^2 = r^2 + t^2$,
(iii) $x^2 + z^2 = IC^2 = r^2 + s^2$.
From assumption (i),
(iv) $y + z = s + t$.
If you substitute (iv) for (ii) - (iii),
(v) $y - z = t - s$.
From (v) and (iv)
(vi) $y = t$, $z = s$.

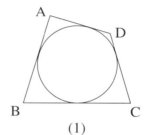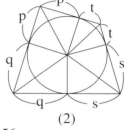

(1) (2)

Fig. 56

If you substitute this for (ii), $x = r$, and the circle comes in contact with side CD. Q.E.D.
This proposition is strange. Even if you decide the lengths of sides of a quadrilateral, the shape is undecided.
Nonetheless, if it has an inscribed circle in certain conditions, the proposition guarantees that it will not lose the property of having an inscribed circle no matter how it is deformed (Figure 58).

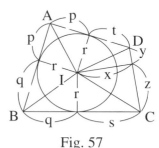

Fig. 57

In Figure 58, three vertexes B, A" and D" are on a straight line. Quadrilateral A"BCD" is no longer a quadrilateral, but a triangle. Quadrilateral A*BCD* is a reentrant quadrilateral, but in the process of transformation from original quadrilateral ABCD, it becomes a triangle once. How should we deal with a triangle like this? Mathematics allows no exceptions.

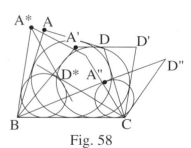

Fig. 58

Definition 4.2 To consider a triangle as a **quadrilateral** by regarding one of the contact points of the inscribed circle as a vertex will be defined as sguarization. The vertex will be called a **flat vertex**. All the salient and reentrant quadrilaterals, which have a sguarized triangle and an inscribed circle, will be called a **quadrilateral with inner center**, and the triangle a **flat quadrilateral with inner centr**.

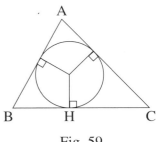

Fig. 59

Proposition 4.3 When triangle ABC is regarded as a quadrilateral with inner center, the following are true.
(vii) It has three candidates for the fourth vertex, or a flat vertex.
(viii) The three vertexes of (vii) are feet of the three perpendicular lines drawn from the center of the inscribed circle.
(ix) Flat vertex H on side BC satisfies BH+CA=AB+HC
This also applies to the other two sides.

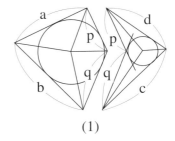

(1)

Joining quadrilaterals, of which two sides match like figure 60, will be called **two-side union**. With regard to such joining as this, the quadrilateral with inner center has a good property.

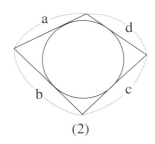

(2)

Fig. 60

Proposition 4.4 The two-side union of a quadrilateral with inner center will also make another quadrilateral with inner center.

Proof In Figure 60 (1), by Proposition 4.2,
(x) a+q=b + p, c+p=d+q
The sum of the two equations
(xi) a+c=b+d
Therefore, it has an inscribed circle by Proposition 4.2. QED. If you apply Proposition 4.4 to a triangle, you will obtain the following proposition.

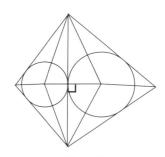

Fig. 61

Proposition 4.5 With regard to the two triangles, which have a side in common, if the feet of the perpendicular lines drawn from the inner centers of the triangles toward the common side are identical, the quadrilateral, which is joined by the two triangles, is a quadrilateral inner center (Figure 61).

4.4 The Generalized Bird Bases

Since preliminaries have been arranged, now let's go on to the main subject.

Definition 4.3 When it is possible to fold quadrilateral ABCD flat on the creases as shown in Figure 62 (1), and the four sides are overlapped on the straight line which runs through point K, Figure 62 (2) will be called the **generalized bird base**, and point K the **(generalized) bird-base center** and the straight line (Figure 62 (3)) the **axis (of generalized bird)**.

The condition that the four sides and one point should be overlapped on a straight line seems to be too strict, but it is indispensable to fold the bird neatly. If sides AB and BC do not overlap, ∠ABC spreads and the reverse of the paper peeps between them (Figure 63 (2)). Supposing sides AB and BC overlap, if point K is off the axis of the bird, either fold AK or CK crosses the slit ABC, and the paper is caught when lifting the neck and tail (Figure 63 (3)).

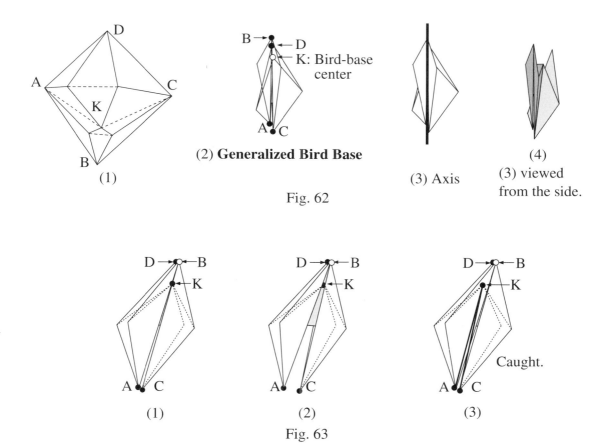

(2) **Generalized Bird Base**

(1)

(3) Axis

(3) viewed from the side.

(4)

Fig. 62

(1)

(2)

(3) Caught.

Fig. 63

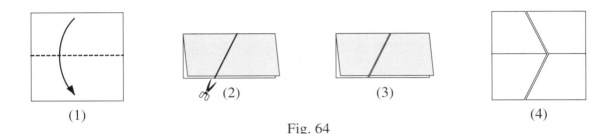

(1) (2) (3) (4)

Fig. 64

Figure 64 illustrates the paper that was folded in half, cut straight and opened. The slits are symmetrical with respect to the fold line. Figure 65 (1) is the generalized bird base that was cut along the axis and opened. It is separated into four parts, P1, P2, P3 and P4. The (2) is those parts joined together. In the same way as Figure 64, the slits are symmetrical with respect to the fold lines. For instance, in part P1 in Figure 65 (3), B'B and B'K are symmetrical with respect to fold line B'I1. This means that fold line B'I1 is the bisector of angle B'. Other fold lines and parts are also the same. As a result, we obtain the following proposition by combining Proposition 4.1.

Proposition 4.6 If you cut the generalized a bird base along the axis, it is separated into four quadrilaterals with inner center, each having a bisection fold of the angle.

Quadrilateral AKCB of Figure 65 (2) is a two-side union of P1 and P2, quadrilaterals with inner center, so it also becomes a quadrilateral with inner center according to Proposition 4.4. In the same way, quadrilateral ADCK is also a quadrilateral with inner center. Since it is possible to make a two-side union with quadrilateral AKCB and quadrilateral ADCK, resultant quadrilateral ABCD also becomes a quadrilateral with inner center. Thus, we obtain the following proposition.

Proposition 4.7 The shape of paper from which we can fold a generalized bird base must be a quadrilateral with inner cente.

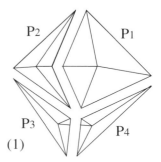

(1)

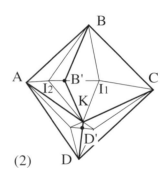

(2)

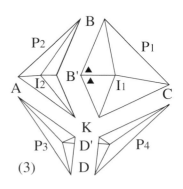

(3)

Fig. 65

It has now become clear that we cannot fold the generalized bird base from paper other than a quadrilateral with inner center. Reversely, can we fold any generalized birds if the shape of paper is a quadrilateral with inner center? It is simple to draw a quadrilateral with inner center. In a circle draw four lines so that they are circumscribed, and try to fold the generalized bird from the paper.

No matter how you may try, you will be unable to fold the paper. The reason is that Proposition 4.7 just mentions 'you cannot fold a generalized bird unless the paper is a quadrilateral with inner center. The generalized bird base consists of the union of four quadrilaterals with inner center, each of which having a bisector.' And it does not introduce any method about how to divide a given quadrilateral with inner center into four quadrilateral with inner centers.

Proposition 4.8 Any quadrilateral with inner center can be divided into two quadrilaterals with inner center by drawing lines between an inside point and two vertexes. The inside point can be put on any place on a hyperbola, which runs through opposite vertexes of the quadrilateral with inner center and its focuses are the other vertexes (Figure 66(1)).

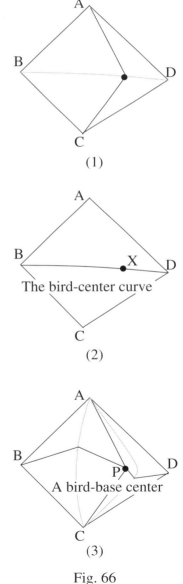

(1)

The bird-center curve

(2)

A bird-base center

(3)

Fig. 66

Proof By Proposition 4.2, quadrilateral ABCD with inner center satisfies the equation, $AB+CD=BC+DA$. It can be expressed as $AB-CB=AD-CD$.
Now let's consider a locus of point X which satisfies the following condition:
(i) $AX-CX=AB-CB (=AD-CD)$.
Since $X=B$ and $X=D$ satisfy (i), the locus of point X becomes the hyperbola which pass through B and D and has focuses, A and C. This will be called **bird-center curve** BD (Figure 66 (2)). Place any point P on the bird-center curve. Point P satisfies (i), so $AP-CP=AB-CB$ and $AP+CB=AB+CP$. By Proposition 4.2, this equation shows that quadrilateral ABCP is a quadrilateral with inner center. Quadrilateral APCD is also a quadrilateral with inner center. Thus quadrilateral ABCD with inner center is divided into two quadrilaterals with inner center. QED.
  If you apply this proposition to two quadrilateral with inner centers, ABCP and APCD, you can obtain four quadrilateral with inner centers
(Figure 66 (3)).
Just draw lines PB and PD to make the second division. In this case, the four triangles are flat quadrilateral with inner centers. And we can obtain the following proposition.

Proposition 4.9 Any quadrilateral with inner center can be divided into four quadrilaterals with inner center.

Now let's fold the quadrilateral with inner center, which was divided into four.

Proposition 4.10 The whole of a quadrilateral with inner center, which was divided into two quadrilateral with inner centers, can be folded flat on the bisector of the angle of each quadrilateral with inner center.

Proof First, cut it (Figure 67 (1)). If you fold each part on the bisector of the angle, the four sides overlap on a straight line as shown by thick lines in (2). The lengths of thick lines (sections) are the same, so they can be joined like (3). Thus you can obtain the quadrilateral with inner center before cutting, which is folded flat. QED.

Figure 68 (1) is quadrilateral with inner centers like Figure 67(4), which are arranged so that you can make a two-side union, and they can be joined on thick lines. If you fold them like Figure 67(3), they become like Figure 68(2), and the thick lines overlap on a straight line. Therefore, they can be joined as proved by Proposition 4.10. The (3) is what is joined, or a generalized bird base. In this way, you can obtain a generalized bird base without fail from a quadrilateral with inner center divided into four (Figure 68 (4)). With Proposition 4.7.

Fundamental theorem 5 It is possible to fold a generalized bird from any quadrilaterals with inner center. In other words, the paper from which a generalized bird can be folded must be a quadrilateral with inner center.

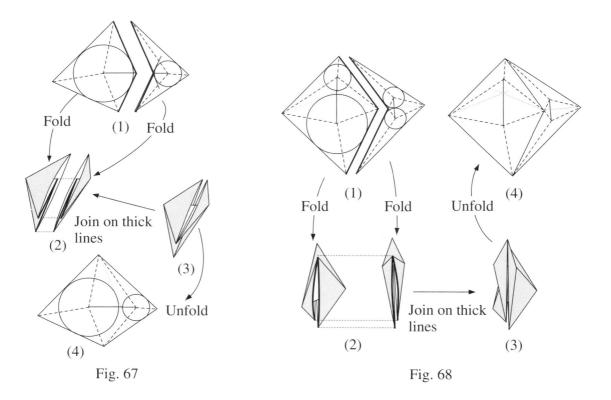

Fig. 67   Fig. 68

4.5 Orizuru Center

In the previous section, an important theorem about the generalized orizuru was given, but Proposition 4.8, the source of the theorem, gives rise to dissatisfaction.

(i) There are two bird-center curves, but only one is used.

(ii) Originally, the four vertexes should be equivalent, but they are not dealt with as such. Now let's look into how (i) and (ii) are reflected in the generalized shape.

Example 4.1 In a square, bird-center curve BD is diagonal line BD. Position bird-base center P on diagonal line BD as shown in Figure 69 (1). The (2) is the development chart of the generalized bird base based on the four divisions of (1). If you make valley folds on dotted lines and mountain folds on solid lines, you can make a generalized orizuru with a large left wing.

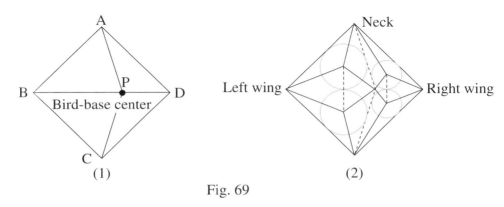

Fig. 69

Following this example, let's make a generalized bird with a long neck. You may think that you can make the bird easily by folding lines of Figure 70 (2), which are drawn on the division of (1). But you are wrong. In (2), the four points marked ● do not fulfill the locally flat folding condition and you cannot fold the paper flat. If you try to fold it flat by force, creases appear like (3), and the upper and lower lines do not join. Anyway, it is impossible to fold it flat. If you stick to the bisection fold of the angle on division of (1), it just becomes Figure 69 (2) rotated 90 degrees, and you cannot make the neck longer. This fact teaches us that if you position the bird-base center on the bird-center curve, both ends of this bird-center curve become the wings.

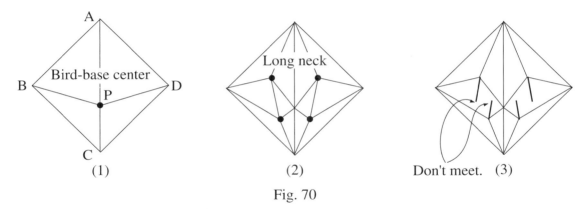

Fig. 70

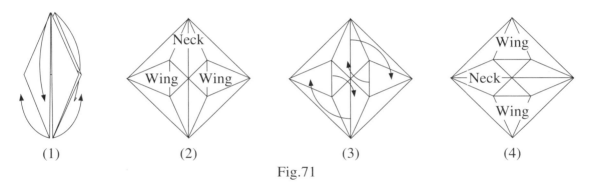

Fig.71

In the ordinary bird base, you can interchange the positions of the neck and tail with wings by moving the corners up and down (Figure 71 (1)). We will call this property the **neck-wing interchangeability**. The exchange of the neck and tail with wings corresponds to the change of fold lines as shown in development charts (2)-(4). In the divisions of Figure 69 (1) and Figure 70 (1), you were unable to exchange the neck and tail with wings. This comes from the unequal treatment of vertexes, (i) and (ii). In other words, you can ensure the neck-wing interchangeability as long as you treat the four vertexes or two bird center curves equally.

Definition 4.4 In a quadrilateral with inner center, the intersection point of the two bird-center curves will be called the **orizuru center**.

Figure 72 (2) is the four divisions of a quadrilateral with inner center by the lines that link the orizuru center and the four vertexes. The orizuru center is on the two bird-center curves, so if you regard it as the point on bird-center curve BD, you can obtain development chart (5). If you regard it as the point on bird-center curve AC, you can obtain development chart (6). If you compare (5) with (6), you can see that the neck-tail and wings are interchanged.

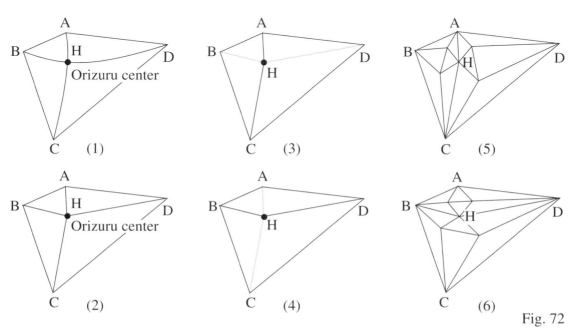

Fig. 72

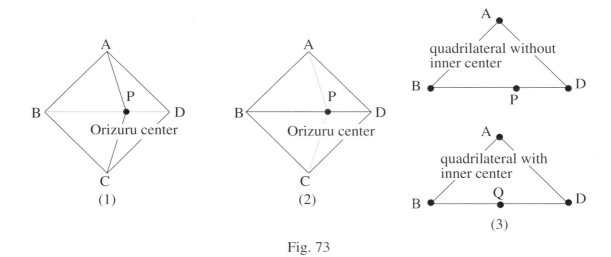

Fig. 73

Now look Example 4.1 (Figure 69) over again with the result in mind. In Figure 73 (1), the square is divided into two left and right quadrilaterals with inner center, but the upper and lower triangles of (2) are not the flat quadrilaterals with inner center. Since the triangles of (2) are not the quadrilaterals with inner center, they cannot be folded like Figure 67 and the whole cannot become a generalized bird. This is the reason why you cannot make wings from A and C, or it has not the neck-wing interchangeability. If we bring the above to a conclusion, it will become as follows:

Proposition 4.11 With regard to Orizuru center H and bird-base center P of the quadrilateral ABCD with inner center, the following are true.

(iii) Bird-base center P is on a bird-center curve, and it can be put in any places.

(iv) When bird-base center P is on bird-center curve BD, and P≠Orizuru center H, quadrilaterals ABCP and CDAP are quadrilaterals with inner center, but quadrilaterals ABHD and CDHB are not. The same is true when bird-base center P is on bird-center curve AC.

(v) Quadrilaterals ABCH, CDAH, ABHD, and CDHB are all quadrilaterals with inner center.

(vi) The generalized bird base with neck-wing interchangeability can be obtained by the bisection fold of the angle made in four triangles ABH, BCH, CDH and DAH.

4.6 The Relations between Husimi's, Justin's and Maekawa's Deformations

First, I will take up **the relation between Husimi's** deformation and a generalized bird made from the paper of kite-shape. Since the kite-shape quadrilateral satisfies the condition of Proposition 4.2 (i), it is a quadrilateral with inner center. Husimi's generalized bird base is a kite-shape quadrilateral to which Proposition 4.11 (v) has been applied (Figure 74).

Yasuji Husimi discovered the method of making an orizuru center by folding paper (Figure 74 (2)).

① Divide the quadrilateral into triangles by an axis of symmetry. Make inner centers in each triangle by the bisection fold of the angle.

② Make a crease which links the inner centers of the triangles. (It is made automatically by ①).

③ The intersection point of the crease of ② and the axis of symmetry is the orizuru center.

Using the method of this book, let's prove why the orizuru center is made by ① - ③. Axis AC is a bird-center curve, so the orizuru center is on the line (Figure 74 (3)). By Proposition 4.11 (v), triangles ABCH and ADCH are flat quadrilateral with inner center and H is the flat vertex of both triangles. By Proposition 4.3 (viii), the flat vertex is the foot of the perpendicular line drawn from the inner centers of both triangles. QED.

Caution: Only the intersection point of diagonal lines of a rhombus becomes the orizuru center. The method of making the orizuru center in a kite-shape quadrilateral was realized through the familiarity with the feature of a quadrilateral with an inscribed circle.

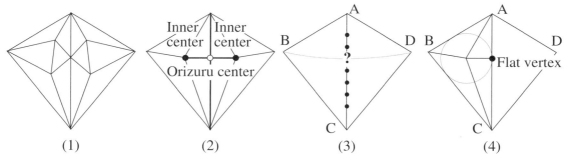

Fig. 74

Frenchman, Jacques Justin advanced Husimi's deformation, and, for the first time, worked out a generalized bird from a salient quadrilateral with an inscribed circle, which has a neck-wing interchangeability. This will be called **Justin's deformation**.

Justin's deformation is Proposition 4.11(v) and (vi) restricted to a salient quadrilateral with inner center. In other words, it is a salient quadrilateral with inner center divided into four triangles by the lines that link the Orizuru center and four vertexes and each is folded on the bisector of the angle. When compared with Proposition 4.11, we can say that Justin's result is part of deformation theories of Orizuru, and it is an orderly and beautiful achievement.

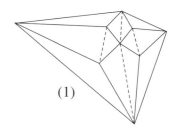

(1)

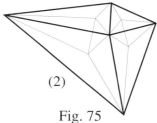

(2)

Fig. 75

Lastly, I will explain **Maekawa's deformation**. Maekawa's deformation uses square paper. The bird-base center is the Orizuru center like Justin's deformation, but it has no neck-wing interchangeability. So far, it seems that it has no points superior to Justin's deformation. But it is not so.

Figure 76 (1) is the development chart of Maekawa's generalized bird base. Although you cannot see from this chart, four divisions of salient and reentrant quadrilaterals with inner center, which are not in Hushimi's and Justin's deformations, are concealed in it (Figure 76 (2)). Maekawa was not aware the quadrilateral with inner center which existed behind, but he discovered the deformation that Hushimi and Justin had overlooked by his excellent sense of origami. Maekawa's deformation applies to a squares, but it also applies to quadrilaterals with inner center. And this deformation can be expressed as 'the four divisions of a quadrilateral with inner center of which vertex is the Orizuru center.'

Figure 77 is a three-dimensional model which illustrates the above. As you can see from the vertical plane of Figure 77, the natural extension of Justin's deformation is to remove the restriction of salient and extend it to a reentrant quadrilateral with inner center or a flat quadrilateral with inner center (triangle). As against it, the dimension of Maekawa's deformation is different. It is applied equally to all the deformations drawn on the vertical plane.

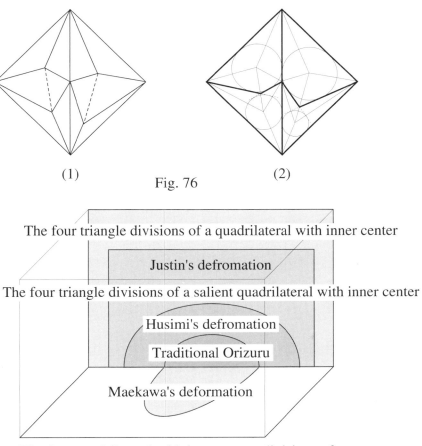

(1)   Fig. 76   (2)

The four triangle divisions of a quadrilateral with inner center

Justin's defromation

The four triangle divisions of a salient quadrilateral with inner center

Husimi's defromation

Traditional Orizuru

Maekawa's deformation

The four quadrilateral with inner center divisions of
a quadrilateral with inner center(Proposition 4.11).

Fig. 77

4.7 Another Concealed Deformation

As referred to in Proposition 4.11, there are some deformations that are hard to make out in Figure 77. That is to shift the bird-base center to points Other than the Orizuru center. Of course you cannot shift the center to any points freely. As mentioned in Proposition 4.11, they must be on the bird-center curve.

By adding what was mentioned in the previous section, we will rewrite Proposition 4.11 as following theorem.

Main theorem 6 (Generalized Bird)
(i) There are three independent deformations.
   a. The deformation of the shape of paper (Husimi's and Justin's deformations)
   b. The movement of the bird-base center (bird-base center≠the Orizuru center)
   c. Bird-base center＝the Orizuru center. The deformation from the two divisions of a quadrilateral with inner center to four divisions (generalized Maekawa's deformation).
(ii) It is possible to fold a generalized Orizuru ⇔ The paper is a quadrilateral with inner center.
(iii) The generalized bird base is a quadrilateral with inner center, which was divided into four, each being folded on the bisector of the angle.
(iv) The common point or bird-base center of the four quadrilaterals with inner center of (iii) can be put on any places on the bird-center curve.
(v) The bird-center curve is a hyperbola, which runs through opposite two vertexes of paper and has its focuses on the other two vertexes.
(vi) The Orizuru center is an intersection point of the two bird-center curves.
(vii) The generalized bird with an neck-wing interchangeability can be obtained from the four triangles divided by the lines which link the orizuru center and the four vertexes.

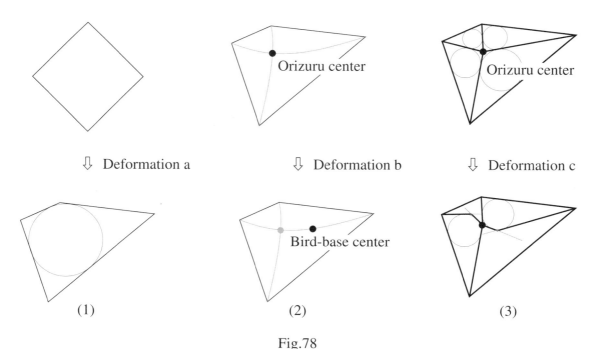

Fig.78

4.8 The Reconsideration of a Quadrilateral With Inner Center

If you fold a sheet of paper flat on the four fold lines which satisfy the locally flat folding condition, cut straight, and open, you can have a quadrilateral with inner center. In this way, you can easily make a quadrilateral for folding a generalized bird. If you cut the paper in a different way, the quadrilateral with inner center changes accordingly. The methods of folding a generalized bird from the salient quadrilateral with inner center (kite-shape quadrilateral) S of Figure 79 (4) and the flat quadrilateral with inner center (triangle) T have already been introduced in section 6. If you bring cut S close to cut R, the quadrilateral with inner center becomes oblong, and the moment when they meet, the lower end opens. The same applies to cut Q.

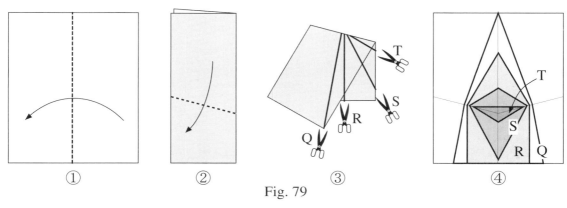

Fig. 79

Open quadrilaterals Q and R have an inscribed circle as shown in Figure 80. Although they are open, we would like to regard them as quadrilaterals with inner center. Can we fold a generalized bird from them? Taking the kite-shape quadrilateral as a model, let's fold the bird from R.

① Divide the quadrilateral by an axis of symmetry and find out the orizuru center (?) by folding one part on the bisector of the angle.

② Link this point and the four vertexes and divide it into four triangles.

③④ Fold each triangle on the bisector of the angle.

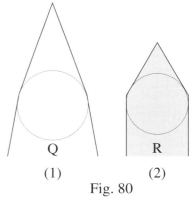

Fig. 80

You can actually fold generalized birds on these creases; from ③, the bird which has symmetry wings and an infinite tail, and from ④, the bird which is symmetry in front and behind and one of the wings is infinite.

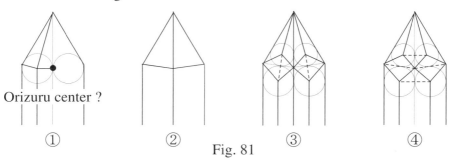

Fig. 81

If you interpret the quadrilateral with inner center broadly like above, you can make unique generalized birds. Examples in Figure 82 do not look like quadrilaterals apparently, but they become quadrilaterals when segmented at the vertexes marked ●. And all the inscribed circles do not seem to contact the four sides. In Figure 82 (1), however, the inscribed circle contact sides a and b at point P, and sides c and d at point Q, so (1) is the quadrilateral with inner center. In the same way, the other quadrilaterals are quadrilaterals with inner center.

If you feel interested, try to fold generalized bird from these **open quadrilateral with inner center** with inner center. First, try to fold **open kite-shape** paper, making use of Husimi's method of making the Orizuru center. Also refer to the charts of Figure 83, which show how to fold generalized bird base without the neck-wing interchangeability from an open irregular quadrilateral with inner center.

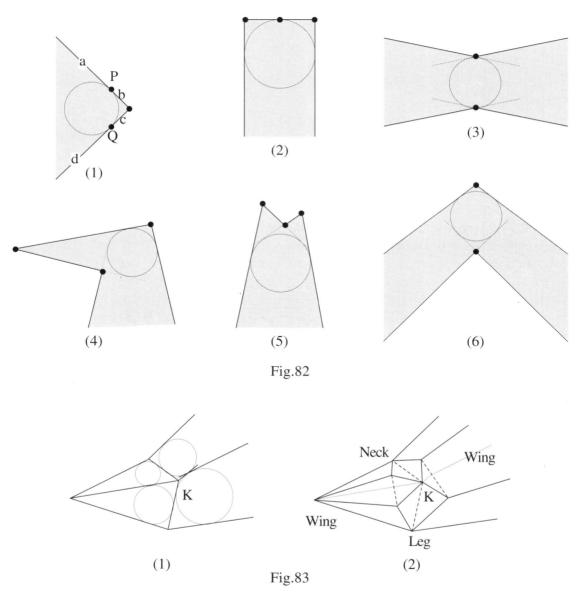

Fig.82

Fig.83

Part Ⅲ The Geometry of Origami

Supplement 4.1 The open quadrilateral with inner center as well as the closed quadrilateral with inner center has the property of becoming a quadrilateral with inner center again when the two side are joined (Proposition 4.4) (Figure 84).

Supplement 4.2 The bird-center curve of an open quadrilateral with inner center includes a parabola, ellipse, circle, straight line besides a hyperbola.

Supplement 4.3 Figure 85 shows the relations of generalized brids with an open quadrilaterals with inner center.

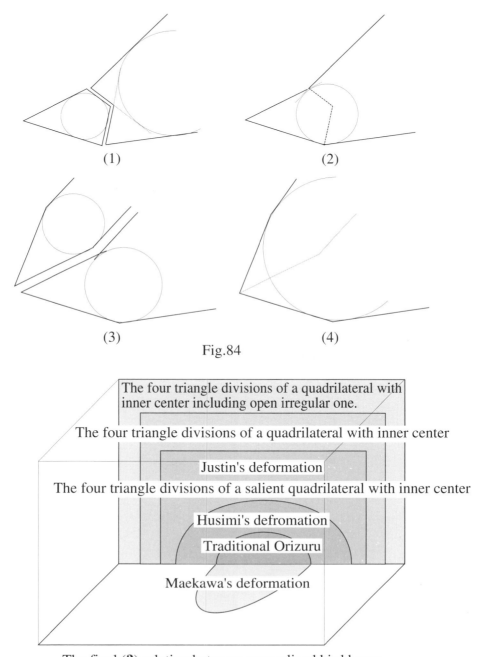

(1)　　　　　　　　　　　　　　(2)

(3)　　　　　　　　　　　　　　(4)

Fig.84

The four triangle divisions of a quadrilateral with inner center including open irregular one.

The four triangle divisions of a quadrilateral with inner center

Justin's deformation

The four triangle divisions of a salient quadrilateral with inner center

Husimi's defromation

Traditional Orizuru

Maekawa's deformation

The final (**?**) relation between generalized bird bases

Fig.85

4.9 Another Reconsideration of Quadrilaterals With Inner Center

Figure 86 shows the variations of an open quadrilateral with inner center (Figure 82 (1)). If the angle of the side increases more than 180 degrees, it becomes a reentrant quadrilateral with inner center like (4), but it is more natural to regard it as (5).

The (5) is identical with (2). This means that you can fold a bird base on the opposite side (outside). If you develop this idea further, you can also fold a generalized bird on the outside of a closed quadrilateral with inner center as shown in Figure 87 ❹.

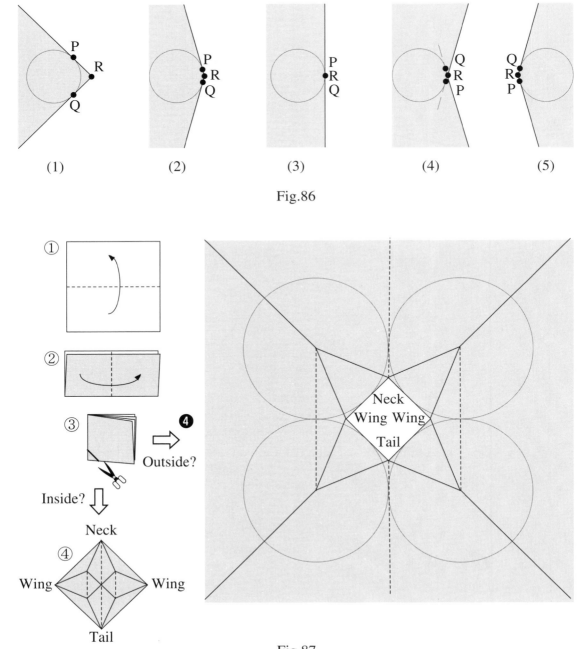

(1)   (2)   (3)   (4)   (5)

Fig.86

Fig.87

4.10 The Spherical Generalized Bird

The possibility of folding a generalized bird on the outside of a quadrilateral with inner center has been explained in the previous section, but the bird in Figure 87 ❹ is a little too strange. Even if we admit the process of Figure 86, it is difficult to accept the idea. However, there are good grounds for folding a bird on the outside besides Figure 86.

Now let's consider the origami with a spherical surface like a balloon (cf. bibliography [Kawa 1]). Fold lines on ordinary paper are straight lines, but the role of straight lines is played by a great circle on a **spherical surface** (figuratively, great circles of a globe are the equator and meridians). Accordingly, if you fold a globe on the equator and let the Northern and Southern Hemispheres overlap, you can obtain a neatly folded spherical surface (Figure 88).

The folding of the whole spherical surface in half on a great circle corresponds to the folding of an infinite flat plane in half on a straight line. In contrast with ordinary origami which uses colored square paper, first of all, we have to make a square on the spherical surface (**spherical square**). Since each side of a spherical square is part of a great circle (**great arc**), if you segment the spherical surface into the four great circles like Figure 90, you can obtain a spherical square. Figure 90 (2) is a hemisphere and we can regard it as a quadrilateral with four vertexes added on the circuit. This hemisphere corresponds to ordinary origami paper or a regular square.

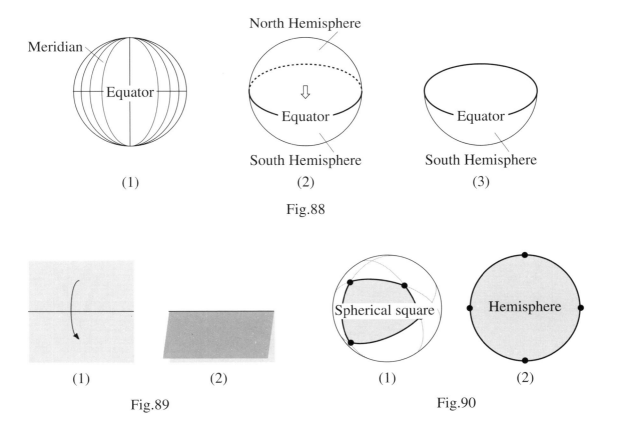

Fig.88

Fig.89   Fig.90

Figure 91 is a spherical bird base based on Figure 90 (2), and it is a perfectly symmetrical generalized bird on a spherical surface. Let's suppose that Figure 91 is the Northern Hemisphere seen from the North Pole. In the previous section, we explored the method of folding a bird on the outside of a quadrilateral with inner center. The outside of the Northern Hemisphere is the Southern Hemisphere, so the bird folded on the outside of Figure 91 is identical with Figure 91. In this way, it is most natural to fold an bird on the outside of a spherical surface.

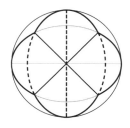

Fig.91

4.11 Applications of a Generalized Bird

Lastly, I introduce three application examples of a generalized bird. Figure 92 (2) is a generalized bird of a quadrilateral with inner center, of which two parts are opened like (3) and (4) in Figure 84. Since the neck and tail of the bird is extremely short, it looks like a turtle. We may call it a **turtle-crane**. In Japan the crane and turtle are symbols of longevity and happiness, so it is a doubly auspicious crane. The turtle-crane can be linked like (3).

Figure 93 is joined two generalized bird bases (with neck-wing interchangeability) of open quadrilaterals with inner center like Figure 82 (6). One of the pleasures of generalized birds is the possibility of linking them like this.

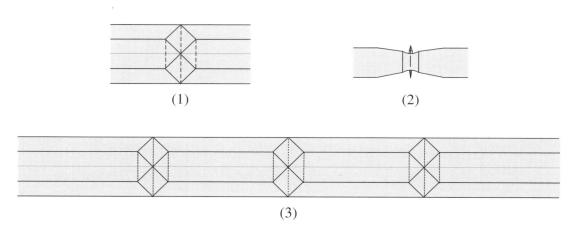

(1)   (2)

(3)

Fig.92

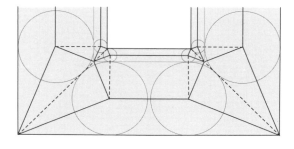

Fig.93

Figure 94 is a combination of an Ordinary orizuru and Figure 82 (1). It is an **airplane Orizuru** with small cranes on both wings, which work as engines. Using the same technique, it is possible to put small cranes midway along the neck and tail.

Practice Fold an airplane Orizuru like Figure 94 from a kite-shape quadrilateral. When completed, it becomes an airplane Orizuru which looks like a Concorde with the wings extended backward.

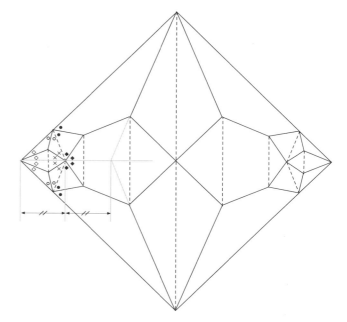

Fig.94

Bibliography

[F] Shuzo Fujimoto, Masami Nishiwaki. Invitation to Creative Origami. Asahi Culture Center (1982)

[Husi] Kouji Husimi, Mitsue Husimi. The Geometry of Origaimi. Nihon Hyoron-sha (1979)

[Huzi] H. Huzita (Editor), ORIGAMI SCIENCE and TECHNOLOGY, Proceedings of the first international Meeting of Origami Science and Technology (1990)

[J] J. Justin, Mathematical Remarks and Origami Bases, Symmetry: Culture and Science, Vol.5, No.2 (1994), pages 153-165

[Kasa] Kunihiko Kasahara, Junsaku Maekawa, Viva Origami, Sanrio (1983)

[Kawa 1] Toshikazu Kawasaki, On Flat Origami of Two-dimensional Spherical Surfaces, a paper submitted to Sasebo Technical Junior College, No. 29 (1992), pages 49-61

[Kawa 2] Toshikazu Kawasaki, Expansions and Their Applications of Systematic Compositions of Cell Decompostions of Flat Origami, - Theories of Deformations of Orizuru, a paper submitted to Sasebo Technical Junior College, No. 32 (1995), pages 29-58

[Mi] K. Miura (Editor), ORIGAMI SCIENCE & ART, Proceedings of the second international Meeting of Origami Science and Scientific Origami (1997)

[Mo] Yoshiei Momotani, Itroduction to Origami, Saito-sha (1974)

[U] Souri Yanagi (Superviso & Editor), Kamonori- The World of Mitsuhiro Uchiyama, Geiun-do

INDEX

ORIGAMI BOOKS
from Japan Publications

3D ORIGAMI: Step-by-step Illustrations by Yoshie Hatahira et.al.
90 pp., 8 1/4 x 10 1/4 in., 24 pp. color, 64 pp. b/w photos and line drawings, paperback.
ISBN: 4-88996-057-0

BRILLIANT ORIGAMI: A Collection of Original Designs by David Brill
240 pp., 7 1/4 x 10 1/4 in., 8 pp. color, 215 pp. line drawings, paperback.
ISBN: 0-87040-896-8

CREATIVE ORIGAMI by Kunihiko Kasahara
180 pp., 8 1/4 x 11 3/4 in., 8 pp. b/w photos, 160 pp. line drawings, paperback.
ISBN: 0-87040-411-3

FABULOUS ORIGAMI BOXES by Tomoko Fuse
98 pp., 7 1/4 x 10 1/4 in., 8 pp. color, 80 pp. line drawings, paperback.
ISBN: 0-87040-978-6

HOME DECORATING WITH ORIGAMI by Tomoko Fuse
126 pp., 7 1/4 x 10 1/4 in., 16 pp. color, 104 pp. line drawings, paperback.
ISBN: 4-88996-059-7

KUSUDAMA: Ball Origami by Makoto Yamaguchi
72 pp., 7 1/4 x 10 1/4 in., 8 pp. color, 65 pp. line drawings, paperback.
ISBN: 4-88996-049-X

KUSUDAMA ORIGAMI by Tomoko Fuse
110 pp., 10 1/8 x 7 1/4 in., 8 pp. color, 81 pp. 2 color line drawings, paperback.
ISBN: 4-88996-087-2

MAGIC OF ORIGAMI, THE, by Alice Gray and Kunihiko Kasahara with cooperation of Lillian Oppenheimer and Origami Center of America
132 pp., 7 1/4 x 10 1/4 in., 122 pp. b/w photos and line drawings, paperback.
ISBN: 0-87040-624-8

ORIGAMI by Hideki Sakata
66 pp., 7 1/4 x 10 1/4 in., 66 pp. full color illustrations, paperback.
ISBN: 0-87040-580-2

ORIGAMI ANIMALS by Keiji Kitamura
88 pp., 8 1/4 x 10 1/4 in., 88 pp. full color illustrations, 12 sheets of origami paper included, paperback.
ISBN: 0-87040-941-7

ORIGAMI BOXES by Tomoko Fuse
72 pp., 7 1/4 x 10 1/4 in., 8 pp. color, 60 pp. line drawings, paperback.
ISBN: 0-87040-821-6

ORIGAMI CLASSROOM I by Dokuotei Nakano
Boxed set, board-book: 24 pp., 6 x 6 in., 24 pp. full color illustrations, plus origami paper: 6 x 6 in., 54 sheets of rainbow-color paper.
ISBN: 0-87040-912-3

ORIGAMI CLASSROOM II by Dokuotei Nakano
Boxed set, board-book: 24 pp., 6 x 6 in., 24 pp. full color illustrations, plus origami paper: 6 x 6 in., 60 sheets of rainbow-color paper.
ISBN: 0-87040-938-7

ORIGAMI FOR PLAYTIME by Satoshi Takagi
158 pp., 6 x 8 1/4 in., 2 color illustrations, paperback.
ISBN: 4-88996-131-3

ORIGAMI FOR THE CONNOISSEUR by Kunihiko Kasahara and Toshie Takahama
168 pp., 7 1/4 x 10 1/4 in., 2 color line drawings, paperback.
ISBN: 4-8170-9002-2

ORIGAMI MADE EASY by Kunihiko Kasahara
128 pp., 6 x 8 1/4 in., 113 pp. b/w photos and line drawings, paperback.
ISBN: 0-87040-253-6

ORIGAMI OMNIBUS: Paper-folding for Everybody by Kunihiko Kasahara
384 pp., 7 1/4 x 10 1/4 in., 8 pp. color, 360 pp. line drawings, paperback.
ISBN: 4-8170-9001-4

ORIGAMI QUILTS
86 pp., 7 1/4 x 10 1/4 in., 8 pp. color, 73 pp. line drawings, paperback.
ISBN: 0-87040-868-2

ORIGAMI TREASURE CHEST by Keiji Kitamura
80 pp., 8 1/4 x 10 1/4 in., full color, paperback.
ISBN: 0-87040-868-2

PAPER MAGIC: Pop-up Paper Craft by Masahiro Chatani
92 pp., 7 1/4 x 10 1/4 in., 16 pp. color, 72 pp. b/w photos and line drawings, paperback.
ISBN: 0-87040-757-0

PLAYFUL ORIGAMI by Reiko Asou
96 pp., 8 1/4 x 10 1/4 in., 48 pp. full color illustrations, 10 sheets of origami paper included, paperback.
ISBN: 0-87040-827-5

POLYHEDRON ORIGAMI FOR BEGINNERS by Miyuki Kawamura
99 pp., 10 1/8 x 8 1/4 in., 51 pp. color, 48 pp. line drawings, paperback.
ISBN: 4-88996-085-6

POP-UP GIFT CARDS by Masahiro Chatani
80 pp., 7 1/4 x 10 1/4 in., 16 pp. color, 64 pp. b/w photos and line drawings, paperback.
ISBN: 0-87040-768-6

POP-UP GEOMETRIC ORIGAMI by Masahiro Chatani and Keiko Nakazawa
86 pp., 7 1/4 x 10 1/4 in., 16 pp. color, 64 pp. b/w photos and line drawings, paperback.
ISBN: 0-87040-943-3

QUICK & EASY MORE ORIGAMI
Boxed set, book: 62 pp., 6 x 6 in., 30 pp. color and 30 pp. line drawings, origami paper: 60 sheets in 6 colors.
ISBN: 4-88996-095-3

Quick & Easy ORIGAMI by Toshie Takahama
Boxed set, book: 60 pp., 6 x 6 in., 30 pp. color and 30 pp. line drawings, origami paper: 60 sheets in 6 colors.
ISBN: 4-88996-056-2

Quick & Easy ORIGAMI BOXES by Tomoko Fuse
Boxed set, book: 60 pp., 6 x 6 in., 30 pp. color and 30 pp. line drawings, origami paper: 60 sheets in 6 colors.
ISBN: 4-88996-052-X

UNIT ORIGAMI: Multidimensional Transformations by Tomoko Fuse
244 pp., 7 1/4 x 10 1/4 in., 8 pp. color, 220 pp. b/w photos and line drawings, paperback.
ISBN: 0-87040-852-6